GLOBE
WORLD
BIOGRAPHIES

D0817238

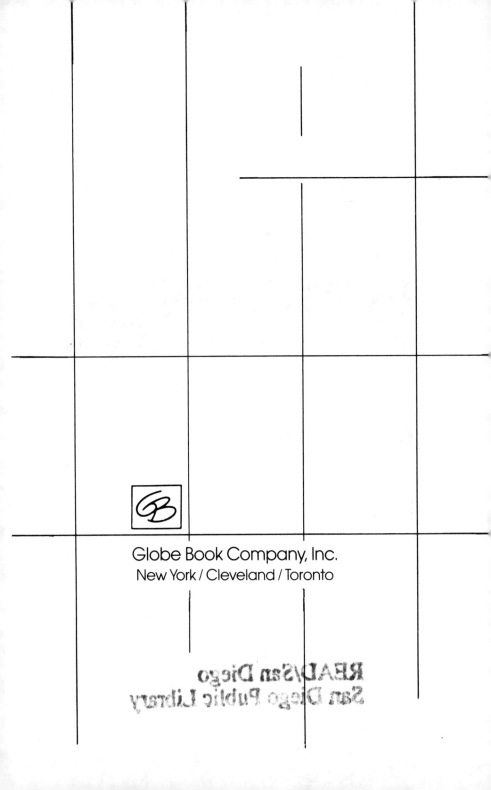

Globe Book Company, Inc.
New York / Cleveland / Toronto

GLOBE

WORLD BIOGRAPHIES

Henry I. Christ

Marie E. Christ
Contributing Author

Henry I. Christ has had a long, distinguished career as a writer, editor, and teacher. A specialist in language, literature, and composition, he is the author of several Globe books, including *Globe American Biographies, Modern Short Biographies, Short World Biographies, The World of Sports, The Challenge of Sports, The World of Careers,* and *Going Places.* In addition to his career as a writer, he is an active member of several professional organizations, and has served as Secretary of the Association of Chairmen in New York City Schools, Vice President of the New York State English Council, and Director of the National Council of Teachers of English. He has spoken at conventions and workshops throughout the United States, lectured on educational television, and frequently participates in curriculum development and evaluation. Henry I. Christ has written many articles for national educational periodicals, and was the editor of *High Points* for nearly 10 years. For the New York State Education Department, he has been a test consultant and a member of various committees on examinations.

Marie E. Christ has worked with Henry I. Christ throughout his career as teacher and writer. She played a major role in the development and preparation of this book.

Editor: Eileen Thompson
Illustrations: Robert Shore
Cover Design: Berg Design
Text Design: Mark Safran

ISBN: 0-87065-039-4

Printed in the United States of America   9 8 7 6 5

Contents

v

To the Student

No topic is more interesting than *people*. What people think about, how they make decisions, and why they act as they do have always been important questions.

In *Globe World Biographies* you will meet 18 different individuals and learn what they have accomplished. This book will give you a glimpse inside their minds, and you will come to understand some of their hopes and fears.

Today's world is rapidly changing. By reading about people who have influenced our world, you'll come to a better understanding of these changes. Each day, you hear about new technological developments—the increasing use of computers, new methods of surgery, pollution control. In this book, you will learn more about these topics.

Each day you also hear news stories about such places as South America, India, and Africa. Some of the men and women in this book have played an important role in these areas of the world.

Sports figures, writers, and performers are often in the news. You will find some old and new friends in *Globe World Biographies*. If you wish, you can continue to read about them in newspapers, books, and magazines.

The questions and other exercises in this book will help you become a better reader. For example, the vocabulary exercises introduce important new words. Each word appears in a sentence that will help you learn its meaning.

Special sections called *Words at Your Service* show you how you can increase your vocabulary by watching for certain clues.

When you have finished *Globe World Biographies* you will know more about people. You will also know more about the world we live in. Happy reading!

UNIT 1

SCIENCE AND THE MODERN WORLD

Genius has the power of lighting its own fire.

JOHN FOSTER

Science dominates our lives. In every area of living, science has a powerful influence. The food we eat, the clothes we wear, the recreations we enjoy are all greatly influenced by science.

Three areas where science is making rapid advances are astronomy, computers, and medicine. Three of the people in this unit made outstanding contributions to these fields.

Edmund Halley, more than 300 years ago, showed that

1

comets are not chance visitors to our solar system. Rather they are members of the solar family that come back to visit us regularly. The comet that visited our skies in 1985–1986 was named for Halley.

Charles Babbage, more than 150 years ago, understood the principle of the computer. He was limited by the materials and knowledge of his time, but he looked forward to an age when computers would play an important role in life.

Daniel Hale Williams was another pioneer. Almost a hundred years ago he performed the first heart operation. He took the first steps toward modern heart surgery, with its transplants and artificial hearts.

There are dangers in the advance of science, too. Rachel Carson was one of the first to point out the danger. She warned the world of the effects of pollution on life and health—and on our very survival.

All four of the following subjects were pioneers. In the history of science, they are giants.

EDMUND HALLEY:
Comet Tamer

*The fault, dear Brutus, is not in our
stars,
But in ourselves. . . .*
WILLIAM SHAKESPEARE

"The comet is coming! The comet is coming!"

In 1985 that message aroused much interest. People looked forward to the arrival of the comet. Astronomers set up tours to far-off places. These were spots where people could best view the comet. Advertisers took advantage of the comet's promised appearance. The word *comet* and pictures of a comet became common in advertisements. For most people there was very little worry.

It was not always that way. Once upon a time the appearance of a comet caused panic. Even the promise of a comet's arrival started all kinds of rumors. The comet would strike the earth. The world would end. Or if the comet missed, there would still be terrible problems. Diseases would spread. Leaders of nations would die or be overthrown. All kinds of troubles would follow.

In the past, comets *inspired* fear and wonder. All over the world the appearance of a comet would cause deep concern. The Incas of Peru, for example, considered comets to be signs of anger from their sun god. The Romans in A.D. 60 thought that a comet signaled the end of Emperor Nero's then six-year-old *reign*.

There is good reason for the excitement caused by a comet. While there are many comets, few are visible to the naked eye. Only a handful in a century are clearly visible. But these naked-eye comets are spectacular.

Nearly everyone knows what a comet looks like. Pictures in books, newspapers, and magazines clearly show the comet's head and long streaming tail. But to see such a sight for yourself on a clear, moonless night is unforgettable.

Comets have appeared in literature and in films. The novelist H. G. Wells imagined a world that passed through the tail of a comet. This meeting had good results. Love and peace spread throughout the land.

This outcome was unusual. Usually literature and

movies predicted the opposite result of such a meeting. In a movie called *Meteor,* a comet threatened to destroy the earth. Russian and American scientists worked together to change the course of the comet. They sent nuclear bombs into space to explode close enough to the comet to *deflect* it, or alter its path. They were generally successful, but pieces from the explosion did reach earth.

There have been other works imagining the arrival of a comet. As long ago as 1857 a book predicted the destruction of the earth by a comet called Donati. The comet actually appeared in 1858. It came from a direction quite different from that of any other comets. Needless to say, Donati missed!

There was one good reason for the terror brought on by comets. No one could predict when they would arrive. They arrived suddenly, without warning. Astronomers could predict all kinds of heavenly events. They could calculate sunrise and sunset, moonrise and moonset. They could tell where, in the heavens, the planets would be at any given moment. But they couldn't predict when comets would arrive.

One of the scariest of all heavenly events used to be the eclipse. When the sun was covered by the moon, ancient people thought the world was ending. To see the light of heaven go out was terrifying. But this event became less frightening in time. Astronomers learned more about the movements of the sun and moon. They could predict when eclipses would begin. They could also predict when the eclipses would end! That kind of knowledge brought relief to worriers.

Comets were different. They seemed to appear from nowhere. They streaked across the sky in one direction around the sun. Then they sped back away and out of the sky. No one could tell when these wanderers would appear. No one—until Edmund Halley.

There are a few names in astronomy that are known to almost everyone. *Halley* is such a name. What makes Edmund Halley so special? Why is his name almost as well known as that of Einstein? Halley helped tame the comets. He made the first accurate prediction about the return of a comet. He suggested that comets are captives of the sun, held in a regular path, not *casual* wanderers from outer space. He gave his name to the most famous of all comets: Halley's comet. Who was this famous astronomer?

Edmund Halley was born in London on October 29, 1656. At the time of his birth, Halley's comet was 26 years away and headed toward the sun. As Halley grew up, the comet kept getting closer and closer. Halley and the comet were headed for a famous meeting.

Meanwhile Halley attended St. Paul's School in London and then Queen's College, Oxford. He became interested in astronomy at an early age. In 1676 he published a paper on the orbits of the planets. He was 20 years old.

In that same year Halley went to the lonely island of St. Helena in the South Atlantic Ocean. It was an ideal spot for observing the stars. The stars in the southern skies are not visible in northern spots like London. Halley, then, was able to see an unfamiliar sky from his post in that southern island. While there, he made a catalog of 341 stars.

A year later, in 1677, he studied the motion of the planet Mercury and added to our knowledge of the sun and planets. He returned to England but kept his interest in the stars and planets alive.

When Halley came back to London, he met Isaac Newton. This was a lucky meeting for both men. Many people consider Newton to be the greatest scientist who ever lived. The two men had much in common. They helped each other develop new and original ideas.

The two men often talked about Newton's theory of gravitation. Newton showed that heavenly bodies influence each other. Gravitation keeps the moon a captive of the earth. Without the force of gravitation, the moon would fly off into space.

All the planets in the solar system are kept in place by the gravitational pull of the sun. Each planet is in a fixed orbit. This orbit balances the speed of the planet with the tug of the sun.

Picture a stone tied to a string. If you whirl the stone about your head, you will be imitating the actions of the planets. The string is like the gravitational pull of the sun. If the string breaks, the stone flies away. The planets do not move around the sun in perfect circles, but the sun holds them in orbit.

"I wonder if the comets are like the planets. I wonder if they are controlled by the sun," Halley thought. When the comet of 1682 appeared, Halley studied it closely. He decided that this comet was not a one-time visitor.

"This comet will return," he declared. By studying its path, he concluded that the comet would return in 1757. To make this prediction, he had to go through complicated calculations. Was Halley right? The comet was actually sighted on Christmas Day, 1758. This was close to the time he calculated. By then Halley had been dead more than 16 years, but his name was attached to the comet. Ever since, Halley's comet has been a regular visitor.

Edmund Halley's work with comets is more important than his other studies. But all his work was interesting. In 1703 he was appointed professor of geometry at Oxford University. In 1720 he became the astronomer royal of England. He helped his friend Isaac Newton with the publication of Newton's greatest work.

Halley was an inventor. He invented a diving bell and

tested it himself. He sailed on a small warship, the *Paramore*. He commanded it for two voyages to the South Atlantic for a study of the earth's magnetic field. On the *Paramore* he also studied the tides in the English Channel.

He was interested in the earth's atmosphere. He climbed a mountain to show how air pressure lessens with height. He mapped the winds of the world. When he was 64 he decided to study the moon through a *cycle* of 18 years. He completed that task. He also pointed out the motion of the stars.

Edmund Halley deserves a place in the history of science for many reasons. But now he is generally known only as the first expert on the orbits of comets.

Let's look more closely at the comet named for him.

Halley's comet returns roughly every 76 years. Since the time of Edmund Halley, the comet has returned on schedule. Though 76 years is a lifetime, some people have seen two appearances of Halley's comet. There are people now alive, for example, who saw the appearance of Halley's comet in 1910 and its return 76 years later. There are people now alive who will see the return of Halley's comet in about 2061, 76 years or so after its appearance in 1985–1986.

Halley's comet has had a long history. Not only is it possible to look into the future of the comet, we can also study its past. The appearance of Halley's comet in centuries past is reported in the history books. But before Edmund Halley, no one realized that the comets of 1531 and 1607 were one and the same.

After Halley, astronomers and historians began to check back into the past. Sure, enough! About every 76 years a bright comet was reported or pictured in art. Halley's comet has been around a long time.

How far back can Halley's comet be traced? Ancient

clay tablets in the British Museum describe a comet in 164 B.C. Scholars say this is Halley's comet. There is even a possible mention of it as far back as 240 B.C. For more than 2,000 years Halley's comet has been keeping its date with earth.

During the years between 240 B.C. and the present, there are many mentions of this great comet. Every appearance of this marvelous sight is recorded somewhere—in Europe, China, and elsewhere. What seemed like a *coincidence* occurred in 1066, as two unusual events took place at the same time. This was the year of the Battle of Hastings and the arrival of Halley's comet. The Norman leader, William the Conqueror, defeated Harold, the king of England. Many people thought that the comet had helped overthrow the English king. A famous picture of the event shows Harold frightened of the comet.

William Shakespeare saw the 1607 appearance. He refers to comets in several of his plays.

Halley's comet is a comfortable visitor. It is visible to the naked eye. It comes back on a regular schedule. The schedule is short enough for one person to see it twice in a lifetime. Mark Twain, the author of *Tom Sawyer,* thought his life was bound up with the comet. He was born in 1835, a year when Halley's comet went by earth. He said he'd probably die the year Halley's comet came back. He was right. Twain died in 1910.

Not all comets are as visible as Halley's comet. About 45 comets return within a ten-year period. One comet returns every 3.3 years. But these comets are not as bright as Halley's. Then there are comets that return only after very long periods. The great comet of 1843 will return after 102,000 years. The great comet of 1864 will not return for about three million years. Halley's comet really is special.

As 1985 approached, great preparations were made for viewing the comet. The comet would be best seen in the Southern Hemisphere. Visitors went on tours to the deserts of Peru and Chile, or to the dry areas of Australia. People were advised to look for Halley's comet on moonless nights, far away from artificial lights.

Some nations planned to send spacecraft for a closer look at our returning relative. Excitement ran high. As the fall of 1985 approached, people began to scan the skies. The best viewing was predicted for the spring of 1986, but many hoped for a look as the comet approached the sun, in 1985.

What would people be looking for? They expected to see a sight that stretched across the sky. They would look for a brilliant head and a long streaming tail, always away from the sun. Like all comets, Halley's comet has little actual substance for its great size.

The tail of a comet may stream off the head for a million miles. Though the tail is long and impressive, it contains very little matter. The head is much smaller than the tail. The center of the head, called the *nucleus,* is smaller still. But how dramatic these elements can be!

As the summer of 1985 changed to fall, people waited. One of the greatest sky shows of all was about to begin.

Were you there? Did you see Halley's comet?

UNDERSTANDING WHAT YOU HAVE READ

Finding Another Title

1. Another good title for this selection might be **(a)** The Appearance of Comets **(b)** Comets as Bringers of Bad News **(c)** The Man Who Explained Comets **(d)** Edmund Halley's Friendship with Isaac Newton.

Getting the Main Idea

2. Comets **(a)** follow the same natural laws as the planets **(b)** frightened people 2,000 years ago **(c)** are usually named for the people who discover them **(d)** were all given names by Edmund Halley.

Finding Details

3. Nero was **(a)** an early astronomer **(b)** a friend of Edmund Halley **(c)** the name of a comet **(d)** a Roman emperor.
4. The comet Donati actually appeared in **(a)** 1657 **(b)** 1682 **(c)** 1857 **(d)** 1858.
5. Edmund Halley studied the motion of the planet **(a)** Mars **(b)** Mercury **(c)** Venus **(d)** Jupiter.
6. "This comet will return" was said by **(a)** Isaac Newton **(b)** Edmund Halley **(c)** Mark Twain **(d)** none of these.
7. After Halley's death, the comet returned in **(a)** 1656 **(b)** 1676 **(c)** 1758 **(d)** 1787.
8. Edmund Halley studied all of the following subjects EXCEPT **(a)** the speed of light **(b)** the earth's atmosphere **(c)** tides in the English Channel **(d)** the earth's magnetic field.

9. Mark Twain (**a**) wrote a story about Halley's comet (**b**) studied the behavior of comets (**c**) died in the year of Halley's comet (**d**) was five years old when Halley's comet appeared in 1835.
10. All of the following were mentioned as good places to see Halley's comet EXCEPT (**a**) Peru (**b**) Australia (**c**) Chile (**d**) New Zealand.

Making Inferences

11. In times past comets were especially terrifying because they were (**a**) common (**b**) brighter than the sun (**c**) mysterious (**d**) close to the planet Mercury.
12. H. G. Wells believed that the arrival of a comet might (**a**) have a good effect (**b**) bring great destruction to earth (**c**) make the sun and the stars seem less bright (**d**) help the study of astronomy.
13. When Halley concluded that the comet would return, he was mainly influenced by his study of (**a**) the southern stars (**b**) Newton's law of gravitation (**c**) the earth's magnetic field (**d**) the planet Venus.
14. Edmund Halley is most famous for his (**a**) study of the comet (**b**) work in listing 341 stars (**c**) help in the publication of Isaac Newton's great work (**d**) study of the 18-year cycle of the moon.
15. The comets that appeared in 1531 and 1607 were actually (**a**) falling stars, not comets (**b**) Halley's comet (**c**) welcomed by the people of the time (**d**) seen by William Shakespeare.

Predicting What Happens Next

16. Halley's comet will probably **(a)** disappear forever after the 1985–1986 visit **(b)** come back again before the year 2000 **(c)** be given a new name after the 1985–1986 appearance **(d)** come back at approximately 76-year intervals many times in the future.

Deciding on the Order of Events

17. The following events are scrambled. Arrange them in proper order, as they happened. Use letters only.
  (a) William Shakespeare sees Halley's comet.
  (b) A comet appears at the time of William the Conqueror's victory over the English king.
  (c) Edmund Halley becomes friends with Isaac Newton.
  (d) Edmund Halley studies the stars in the southern skies.

Inferring Tone

18. When Edmund Halley said (7), "This comet will return," he probably spoke with **(a)** doubt **(b)** a sense of humor **(c)** confidence **(d)** sadness.

Separating Facts from Opinions

For each of the following, tell whether the statement is a fact (*F*) or an opinion (*O*).

19. Edmund Halley's discovery was the greatest finding of the seventeenth century.

20. A comet has a tail, a head, and a nucleus.

Understanding Words from Context

21. The Romans in A.D. 60 thought that a comet signaled the end of Emperor Nero's then six-year-old *reign*.
Reign (4) means (a) life (b) period of power (c) impressive appearance (d) election.

22. They sent nuclear bombs into space to explode close enough to the comet to *deflect* it, or alter its path.
Deflect (5) means (a) approach (b) record (c) turn aside (d) photograph.

23. He suggested that comets are captives of the sun, held in a regular path, not *casual* wanderers from outer space.
Casual (6) means (a) important (b) harmful (c) not dangerous (d) not regular.

24. When he was 64, he decided to study the moon through a *cycle* of 18 years.
Cycle (8) means (a) regular period of time (b) change (c) series of observations (d) appearance in the sky.

25. What seemed like a *coincidence* occurred in 1066, as two unusual events took place at the same time.
In *coincidences* (9) (a) nobody is ever surprised (b) two unrelated events happen together (c) there are always disagreements (d) people say and do foolish things.

THINKING IT OVER

1. Strange and mysterious events or objects often frighten us. Why?
2. Why were comets so frightening in the years before Edmund Halley?

3. Have you ever been frightened of something at first? Then when that something was explained to you, did you lose your fear? Tell about your feelings.
4. Some people feel that giving something mysterious a name makes it less frightening. For example, by naming a strange new disease, people seem to gain control over it. How do you feel about the power of names?
5. Did you see Halley's comet? What feelings did you have as you observed this spectacle?
6. Why was Isaac Newton so important to Halley?
7. How did Edmund Halley show his interest in many scientific studies?
8. Have you ever seen a movie in which a comet plays a part in the action? Tell about it. (The movie *Meteor,* for example, might be seen on reruns.)
9. Many amateur astronomers have discovered comets and have had the comets named for them. Why don't scientists using the really big telescopes spend more time searching for possible comets?

ANOTHER LOOK AT THE QUOTATION

> *The fault, dear Brutus, is not in our stars,*
> *But in ourselves. . . .*
> WILLIAM SHAKESPEARE

1. Explain the quotation in your own words.
2. How did people in earlier years blame comets for their misfortunes? Give some examples from the chapter.
3. Why do people like to blame others for their misfortunes and not themselves?
4. Do you believe that the stars influence your actions? How can you be sure?

WORDS AT YOUR SERVICE—WHAT IS CONTEXT?

> *In the past, comets* inspired *fear and wonder. (4)*

Even if you are not sure of the word *inspired,* the sentence gives you a good deal of help. The structure of the sentence tells you that comets are linked with *fear* and *wonder.* By taking an easy step further, you can decide that *inspired* here means *brought on, caused.* Comets *brought on* feelings of fear and wonder. Even if *inspired* is a completely unfamiliar word, you can make an intelligent guess at its meaning.

All the words surrounding *inspired* are called its *context.* The words around unfamiliar words provide excellent clues to word meanings. In this chapter and later ones, you'll explore context as a guide to meaning. The chapters will explain how you can use all the words in a sentence to learn the meaning of a new word.

Context may involve real experiences as well as words. You learned many words as a child by this method. "Here's your milk" taught you the word *milk.*

You are still learning by this method. If someone hands you an object and says, "Try these binoculars," you soon learn what binoculars are.

You have learned many new words by context in reading and listening. Suppose you read, "That subject is highly *controversial.* There are two strong opposing viewpoints about it." If there are two strong opposing sides, you know that *controversial* means *open to argument.*

Context doesn't always give clues. In a sentence like the following, context isn't of much help:

Jerry saw an armadillo.

But if the sentence were like this, it would be of help:

> *As an* armadillo *looked for insects among the leaves, its armor plates glistened.*

The second sentence suggests that an armadillo is an insect-eating animal with armor plates.

When you meet a new word, look at the words around it. You can probably make a good guess at its meaning. These chapters will help you do so.

Study the following sentences and then guess at the meaning of each *italicized* word. Use the entire sentence to help you.

EXAMPLE

During a *calamity,* people often grow closer and face the dangers together.

Calamity means (a) show (b) rainfall (c) disaster (d) interruption.

The sentence tells us that people face dangers together. Danger suggests disaster. The correct answer is (c) *disaster.*

1. Jerry *scoffed* at Julio's plan for a picnic and proposed an entirely different one himself.

   Scoffed means (a) scorned (b) supported (c) repeated (d) reported.

2. The *mural* on one inside wall of the school shows a scene from our early history.

   A *mural* is a (a) kind of clock (b) window frame (c) drapery (d) wall painting.

3. If I am not *hampered* by interruptions, I'll finish my report by ten o'clock.

   Hampered means (a) called (b) bothered (c) aroused (d) supported.

4. Loni's diet will be a success, for she has the *discipline* to stop eating rich foods.
   Discipline means (a) self-control (b) rules (c) unwillingness (d) punishment.
5. At the class spaghetti dinner, dress should be informal but *appropriate*.
   Appropriate means (a) serious (b) proper (c) vivid (d) simple.

CHARLES BABBAGE:

A Man Ahead of His Time

*To do what is impossible for talent is
the mark of genius.*

HENRY F. AMIEL

The computer has changed the world. Almost everything you do is affected by the computer. Computers at check-out counters at the supermarket "read" the products, charge you, and total your bill. Some have voices telling you prices as they are read. Computers at banks keep track of your accounts. Computers for the airlines check your reservations. Computers at libraries keep track of books. Individuals use computers too, to store important information. These are but a very few uses of simple computers. The more complicated computers go beyond our ability to explain.

How do computers work? A computer is a type of calculating machine. Consider the common pocket calculator. It can add, subtract, multiply, divide, and *derive* square roots in an instant. Many calculators can store information for later use. Some calculators fit on wrist watches. Others slip into wallets with ease.

These remarkable machines use tiny elements called *silicon chips*. Chips no bigger than a fingernail can do as much work as huge computers did just a few years ago. Jack Kilby and Robert Noyce, two American inventors, are responsible for the use of silicon chips. The two men, each on his own, came up with the idea that has made the small, complicated computer possible.

Kilby and Noyce made their great inventions in 1958–1959. But their work was aided by the findings of an earlier man. A hundred years before their contributions, a man was working on the problem of the calculating machine. He spent a lifetime trying to solve the problem, but he never reached his goal. Yet he showed the way for others to follow.

Charles Babbage foresaw the wonderful possibilities of calculating machines. He understood the principles that later machines would use. But he didn't have electricity and he didn't have the materials he needed for such a machine. He spent his life building large, complicated machines. His mind ran ahead of his materials. He knew what he needed, but he couldn't get it. Although he is called the "father of the computer," few people know his name. This is his story.

Charles Babbage was born December 26, 1792, in Devonshire, England. Part of his power of concentration may have come from his remarkable mother. She influenced him and encouraged him throughout his life. Once when Babbage was *disheartened* about his work, his mother urged him on. She said, "My advice is to *pursue* it, even if it should oblige [force] you to live on bread and cheese."

Babbage was an unusual young man. Once he was almost hit by a falling piece of slate. He was not alarmed. He picked up the slate, examined it, and called it a fine example of its kind.

Babbage entered Trinity College in 1810. He found his teachers uninterested. He had to teach himself. He formed a society of friends who were interested in mathematics and scientific subjects.

Once a friend found him daydreaming with a book of mathematical tables before him. "Well, Babbage," the friend said, "what are you dreaming about?"

Babbage replied, "I am thinking that all these tables might be calculated by machinery."

Remember that this was more than 150 years ago. No one thought a machine could do calculations. The very idea seemed crazy! This idea was the first sign of the direction that Babbage's life was to take.

Babbage met his future wife, Georgiana Whitmore, at Cambridge University. They were married in June 1814, when he received his college degree. He was 21 and she was 20. It was a sad marriage. They had eight children in 13 years. Only three of the children lived to adulthood. Georgiana herself died at age 35.

The marriage was hard for Georgiana. Charles took no responsibility for the children. He was a genius with great energy, but he was a hard man to live with. When the children cried, his wife had to get them out of his way. He became a distant figure feared by his children. He would have been shocked if anyone had told him about his failings.

When his children were still small, he began to work on his machine. But he was interested in other projects too. He noticed how expensive it was to send parcels from one town to another. He suggested that the post office take over the job. He also suggested a simple rate of postage for letters. His ideas were used years later when Great Britain printed the world's first postage stamps.

His mind was forever active. He did experiments to learn more. He went down in a diving bell in Plymouth in 1818. He then wrote an article on diving for an encyclopedia. He foresaw the possible wartime uses of submarines.

He also met some of the great men of the period. He knew the Marquis de Laplace, Sir John Herschel, and Sir Humphry Davy. These men respected him in turn.

In June 1822 he announced that he was making a machine for calculating. Machines had already been invented for doing the physical labor of many people. Babbage's machine would do the mental work of many people. He had a small machine built and challenged men to beat it. The experts could keep up with simple tasks, but soon the machine left them behind. The machine of wheels, bars, and springs just didn't get tired.

It was a long way from this first simple machine to a more effective, larger one. Babbage planned to build a larger machine. He presented his idea to the British government in April 1823. He was so *persuasive* that he received a grant of 1,500 pounds (British dollars) to build the machine. This seemed like a lot of money at the time, but it was really far too little.

There had been simple calculating machines before. The old Chinese abacus is a kind of adding machine. But Babbage's machine would work on an entirely different principle.

Babbage gave himself two to three years to build his machine. It would take him a lifetime and still not be completed! As his biographer Maboth Moseley writes, "A thousand *obstacles* lay in his path." And no one could help him in setting up the processes.

He was in a new area. He had no knowledge of tool-making or metalworking. He realized that he would have to invent many of the tools himself. He even invented a language of signs as aids to memory. As he went on, he made changes. They were improvements, but they took time. They delayed the work.

The year 1827 was one of tragedy. The machine was draining Babbage's energies. Then he lost his father, his wife, and two children. He had a nervous breakdown and went abroad to recover.

The machine was as far from completion as ever. Some scientists said the machine would never work. Babbage returned from his tour. He was discouraged, but he refused to quit.

In 1829 he received a second grant of 1,500 pounds from the government. His cause was helped by the great duke of Wellington, victor over Napoleon. Babbage would soon spend this money. Then he would have to dig into his own funds over and over again.

He ran into difficulties with other scientists. He wasn't an easy man to live with at home. He wasn't easy to get along with in public either. He was fault-finding, sharp-tongued, and sometimes bitter.

He decided to run for Parliament in 1832, but was

badly beaten. His personality didn't help. In spite of his disappointment, he kept working on his machine, improving and improving but never finishing it.

The machine sometimes *depressed* him. But instead of letting his disappointment defeat him, he worked on other things. He improved methods of banking. He thought up ways to uncover forgeries. He looked at the safety problems on trains. He observed the pin-making industry and the printing trade. He studied insurance records and improved insurance tables. He wrote a ballet and invented colored lighting for the stage. He would have written a novel, but a friend talked him out of it. He invented the ophthalmoscope, an instrument for examining the eye.

Babbage became very good friends with Lady Ada Lovelace, the daughter of the famous poet Lord Byron. She was a very intelligent woman and was interested in Babbage's machine. She understood the machine and his aims. In a long series of letters, she encouraged him and gave him her own ideas.

In 1846 he applied for a government post. He hoped in this way to earn more money for his machine. But he did not get the job. He became more bitter than ever.

In 1855 a Swiss inventor made a calculating machine based on Babbage's work. Babbage was generous and helped him win honors for the invention.

The finished part of Babbage's machine was shown at an exhibition in 1862. It was not well displayed. As Maboth Moseley reports, "There was very little light, and the machine could be seen by no more than six people at a time." The machine continued to be misunderstood and neglected.

Why was the machine never truly finished? An old French proverb says, "The best is the enemy of the good." In other words, sometimes we must make use of the good while we still strive for the best. Babbage never finished the machine because he was never satisfied. He seemed too much taken by plans and drawings. He would take a practical step forward and then make changes in what he had already done.

Babbage's last years were not happy. He died at age 79, on October 18, 1871. His work was never completed.

Some inventors built on his ideas. Herman Hollerith, for example, invented a card-punch machine that helped found the parent company of today's IBM. It wasn't until a hundred years after Babbage's death that the computer became a necessary part of everyday life.

Babbage was a hundred years too early. Suppose he had been born in the twentieth century. Who knows what he might have done? He spent his life on a dream that never quite came true. His machines are not lost, however. His son Henry gave them to the Science Museum in London. Perhaps some day you will see these machines. The work of these giant machines can now be done easily by a silicon chip smaller than a dime.

UNDERSTANDING WHAT YOU HAVE READ

Finding Another Title

1. Another good title for this selection might be **(a)** Modern Computers **(b)** The History of Computers **(c)** The Father of the Computer **(d)** Computers a Hundred Years Ago.

Getting the Main Idea

2. Charles Babbage (a) couldn't finish his machine with the materials of the time (b) invented a machine for examining the eye (c) was a gentle, lovable person (d) was a lazy person who lost interest in his machine.

Finding Details

3. The silicon chip was invented by (a) Charles Babbage and Jack Kilby (b) Robert Noyce and Sir John Herschel (c) Jack Kilby and Robert Noyce (d) Charles Babbage and Sir John Herschel.
4. The person who gave Charles the advice to "live on bread and cheese" if he had to was his (a) son (b) father (c) wife (d) mother.
5. Charles Babbage earned his college degree (a) at the age of 18 (b) the year he received a government grant for his machine (c) in 1810 (d) the year he married Georgiana.
6. The first postage stamps were printed by (a) the United States (b) France (c) Germany (d) Great Britain.
7. The duke of Wellington (a) was the uncle of Lady Ada Lovelace (b) helped Babbage get a government grant (c) had been defeated by Napoleon (d) was prime minister of England.
8. Charles Babbage ran for a seat in Parliament in (a) 1827 (b) 1832 (c) 1846 (d) 1855.
9. Charles Babbage did all the following EXCEPT (a) write a ballet (b) improve methods of banking (c) study insurance records (d) write a novel.
10. Lady Ada Lovelace was (a) a daughter of Lord Byron (b) a novelist (c) an enemy of Charles Babbage (d) the second wife of Charles Babbage.

Making Inferences

11. If Babbage had had electricity, **(a)** he would have invented the electric typewriter **(b)** his work would have been easier **(c)** Sir John Herschel would have formed a partnership with him **(d)** he would have lost interest in a calculating machine.

12. Babbage's treatment of his family probably came from **(a)** kindness **(b)** satisfaction with his life outside the home **(c)** lack of understanding **(d)** dislike of his wife.

13. Babbage's children probably feared him because **(a)** he was a scientist **(b)** their mother loved him **(c)** he didn't spend enough time with them **(d)** they were not very intelligent.

14. In working on his machine, Babbage was probably most encouraged by **(a)** Lady Ada Lovelace **(b)** his wife **(c)** his father **(d)** his son Henry.

15. It may truly be said that Charles Babbage **(a)** had many interests **(b)** was a soft-spoken man **(c)** invented the light bulb **(d)** completed the machine in the two or three years he planned for it.

Predicting What Happens Next

16. If Charles had lived five more years, he probably would have **(a)** won a huge grant from the British government **(b)** invented an effective storage battery **(c)** married a second time **(d)** continued to work on his unfinished machine.

Deciding on the Order of Events

17. The following events are scrambled. Arrange them in proper order, as they happened. Use letters only.

(a) Charles marries Georgiana.
(b) Charles enters Trinity College.
(c) Part of his machine is put on display at an exhibition.
(d) Charles runs for a seat in Parliament.

Inferring Tone

18. On page 24 Maboth Moseley reports on the display of Babbage's machine at an important exhibition. Her tone is one of (a) great joy (b) simple satisfaction (c) boredom (d) sadness.

Separating Facts from Opinions

For each of the following, tell whether the statement is a fact (*F*) or an opinion (*O*).
19. Babbage's machine did not have the help of modern science.
20. Babbage was a greater inventor than Thomas Edison.

Understanding Words from Context

21. It can add, subtract, multiply, divide, and *derive* square roots in an instant.
    Derive (20) means (a) obtain (b) repeat (c) pass over (d) try out.
22. "My advice is to *pursue* it, even if it should oblige [force] you to live on bread and cheese."
    Pursue (21) means (a) describe (b) turn down (c) follow (d) tell about.
23. He was so *persuasive* that he received a grant of 1,500 pounds to build the machine.
    Persuasive (22) means (a) sweet (b) happy (c) intelligent (d) convincing.

24. It would take him a lifetime and still not be completed. As his biographer Maboth Moseley writes, "A thousand *obstacles* lay in his path."
Obstacles (23) means **(a)** new opportunities **(b)** stumbling blocks **(c)** tricky enemies **(d)** uncertainties.

25. The machine sometimes *depressed* him. But instead of letting his disappointment defeat him, he worked on other things.
Depressed (24) means **(a)** saddened **(b)** influenced **(c)** encouraged **(d)** angered.

THINKING IT OVER

1. What were Charles Babbage's strongest qualities? What were his weakest? How did all these qualities affect his progress?

2. In a short story, Stephen Vincent Benét made an interesting point. He said that Napoleon would have died unknown if he had been born a few years earlier. Do you believe that the times make the person? Or does a person make the times? Explain. Would Charles Babbage have been a great inventor if he had been born a hundred years later?

3. You may feel that Charles Babbage's wife, Georgiana, had an unfair share of the family burdens. Has the life of women improved in recent years? Explain.

4. How did Charles Babbage's unpleasant personality lose him friends?

5. Some people feel that learning generally stops when school is over. Others say that school prepares us to learn. The rest is up to us. Explain how you feel.

6. How did Babbage show a willingness to keep learning?
7. When a person has a good idea, why isn't the idea always accepted immediately?
8. How has your life been influenced by the use of the silicon chip?

ANOTHER LOOK AT THE QUOTATION

> *To do what is impossible for talent is the mark of genius.*
>
> HENRY F. AMIEL

1. Explain the quotation in your own words.
2. Was Charles Babbage a genius? Or was he just talented? Explain.
3. Which is rarer in the world, talent or genius? Explain.
4. Give an example of someone you consider a genius and of a person of great talent.
5. Have you ever succeeded in a task you first considered impossible? Tell about it.

WORDS AT YOUR SERVICE—THE SENTENCE AS A WHOLE

> *Once when Babbage was* disheartened *about his work, his mother urged him on. (21)*

Even if *disheartened* is a new word to you, the sentence provides the clues you need to figure out its meaning. In the previous chapter you learned that a word's context is its surrounding words. Here, the entire sentence gives you a clue to the meaning of *disheartened.* If Babbage needed urging, he must have been discouraged. *Discouraged* is a good guess for *disheartened.*

Study the following sentences and then guess at the meaning of each *italicized* word. Use the entire sentence to help you.

EXAMPLE

The old shack was *dilapidated,* with shutters hanging loose and the roof crumbling.

Dilapidated means (a) spick and span (b) falling apart (c) newly painted (d) rusty.

If the shutters are loose and the roof is crumbling, the shack must be (b) *falling apart.*

1. When Dotty heard the good news, she was *jubilant.*
   Jubilant means (a) bored (b) unhappy (c) joyful (d) weary.
2. If there are any *omissions* in your report, please fill in the missing items later.
   Omissions are (a) ink spots (b) lies (c) items left out (d) items copied from elsewhere.
3. Even though he faced misfortune, Grant overcame his *desperation* and looked ahead with hope.
   Desperation means (a) hopelessness (b) strange sense of humor (c) cruel manner (d) hatred.
4. When you solve a problem, you should consider all the elements of the problem in *sequence,* one point at a time.
   Sequence means (a) haste (b) a short time (c) your own way (d) order.
5. Nan cannot play tennis, but she obtains *sufficient* satisfaction from watching the matches on television.
   Sufficient means (a) not any (b) enough (c) unpleasant (d) impossible.

RACHEL CARSON:
Guardian of the Environment

I truly believe that the fundamental [basic] principles of ecology govern our lives, wherever we live, and that we must wake up to this fact or be lost.

KARIN SHELDON

You don't live in a world cut off from nature. You are not a mechanical object. You are a part of nature. Your body operates according to the laws of nature. The air you breathe is provided by natural processes. The food you eat depends upon the farmer's cooperation with nature. You are part of a very complicated network of other people and natural forces. You are affected by the events that happen to this great network.

The world and the people around you are your environment. If something harmful is done to that environment, you can suffer. Natural disasters like earthquakes can affect that environment in an unpleasant way. Even lesser problems can affect you. A heavy freeze in Florida, for example, may cause you to pay more for oranges and vegetables.

Natural disasters usually cannot be avoided. Earthquakes, tornadoes, drought, flooding, hurricanes, and volcanic eruptions are all part of the world we live in. But human beings have added many problems of a different kind.

Many disasters are caused by human beings. As we progress in some areas, we make other things a lot worse. We pollute the air and water. We add possibly harmful chemicals to foods in order to preserve them. We kill off animal species that can contribute to our lives.

Not long ago only a handful of people knew the word *ecology*. Now the word appears often in newspaper and television reports. *Ecology* means the study of living things in the vast network of life. Every living thing exists in relation to its environment and to other living things. Nothing exists all by itself.

Here's an example. In a natural setting, wolves and deer live in relation to each other. Left alone, the deer may become too numerous. They may eat up their food supply and begin to die of hunger. The wolves act as a natural balance. By keeping the deer population down, they actually help the deer herd. They kill off the weakest members. The strongest can survive because more food is available. The strongest pass on their strength to their offspring. If the herds get too small, the wolf population also gets smaller. The two species are directly tied to each other.

The deer-wolf illustration is a simple one, but it shows how individual parts of nature work together. If human beings step in and upset the balance, trouble may result. If we kill off harmless snakes, rats and mice may get out of control. If we kill off birds, insects may get out of control. If we kill off the animal hunters, the hunted may die of starvation.

There are other ways in which we can tamper with nature. During World War II, the chemical DDT proved effective against all kinds of insects. It was widely used, but then some harmful side effects began to show up. DDT got into the bodies of fish. The ospreys, or fish eagles, ate the fish. The DDT got into the bodies of the ospreys. The eggs they laid had soft shells. Many failed to hatch. Ospreys began to disappear.

There were other unexpected side effects. DDT proved harmful to human beings. Then the chemical became less effective in doing the job it was designed for. Many insects developed *immunity* to DDT. Some individual insects were not killed by it. These insects bred a generation of insects that could not be killed by the chemical. People had to take another look at the use of DDT.

So the story goes on. In an effort to improve life, we sometimes do harmful things. For short-term gains we sometimes sacrifice more important long-range safety. We need to examine the entire picture before we go too far in any one direction.

In recent years the government has become concerned

about pollution. On December 2, 1970, it set up the Environmental Protection Agency. This agency tries to protect us from projects that would injure the world we live in. It is concerned with all threats to the environment. If, for example, a large apartment house is going to be built near the shore, the Environmental Protection Agency, or EPA, will look at the possibility of beach destruction. The EPA does many other things. It studies the gasoline used in automobiles. It tries to prevent the release of harmful chemicals into American rivers.

We have moved in the right direction and made great *strides* in protecting the environment. But it wasn't always that way. After World War II, the growth of American industry brought all kinds of problems. Air and water pollution increased dangerously. Thoughtless use of chemicals was destroying the balance of nature. The network of life was being threatened. Not much was being done about this dangerous development.

One individual can make a difference. At the moment when environmental destruction was at its worst, a mild-mannered woman came along. Her name was Rachel Carson. Almost singlehandedly she made the American public aware of the dangers ahead. Her work aroused the country and forced Congress to act. This is her story.

Rachel Carson was born on May 27, 1907, in Springdale, Pennsylvania. In childhood she developed a deep love of nature. Her mother, Maria Carson, encouraged this love. As a little girl, Rachel observed the farm animals—the pigs, chickens, cows, and horses. But she also studied raccoons and opossums, birds and butterflies, ants and crickets.

Rachel was very much interested in English, especially writing. But in college she came under the influence of an outstanding science teacher. Rachel changed her major from English to biology. She never lost her love of English, though. Later, in her writing, she combined her two interests.

Rachel had a keen sense of fun. Once she took part in an all-star hockey game in college. The opposing teams called themselves Army and Navy. Rachel was the Navy goalkeeper. The goat is a symbol of the Navy team and is supposed to bring it good fortune. Someone suggested getting a goat as a *mascot* for Rachel's team.

Rachel volunteered to get one. She got *two* goats, a nanny and her kid. Near the field she handed the leash rope to Betty MacColl, the official goat-keeper for the day. The nanny goat wanted to get to her kid, so Betty tied the goat to a tree. The goat ran circles around the tree, and Betty was tied to the trunk. Rachel laughed and rescued poor Betty. Later the goat butted one of the cheerleaders.

Rachel graduated and returned home to Springdale for a visit. She was shocked by what she saw. Her native countryside was being spoiled. The valley of the Allegheny River was heavily polluted, and the river itself was very dirty. She began to think about the problem of pollution and the destruction of natural beauty.

She earned a year's scholarship to Johns Hopkins University, in Baltimore. Before she attended, that summer she studied at Woods Hole in Massachusetts. This is a marine research laboratory. She became interested in sea life and wanted to be a marine biologist. At this time she met Elmer Higgins at the U.S. Bureau of Fisheries. He was to become an important influence in her life.

Higgins told her that there were few jobs for women in marine biology. There were occasional openings in teaching and in government work. But most private firms just didn't hire women for this kind of work.

In October 1929 the stock market crashed. The Great Depression began. Money was scarce. To stay in school,

Rachel got a job as a teaching assistant at the Johns Hopkins summer school. In the fall she had a job as lab assistant to Dr. Raymond Pearl. She was also a full-time student. Her special subject was catfish.

She later got a job as lab assistant to Professor C. J. Pierpont. When she received her master's degree in June, she was desperate for a job. She applied to Elmer Higgins. Fortunately, his department had to prepare some scripts for radio programs on fishing and marine life.

Higgins gave Rachel a trial assignment. The script she wrote was excellent. Higgins gave her other scripts to do. Meanwhile a civil service examination came along. It was for a junior biologist in the department. The only woman taking the exam, Rachel also scored the highest. She was appointed as a full-time permanent employee. Her worst money worries were over.

Rachel's radio scripts were turned into a department pamphlet. Higgins asked her to write an introduction. After she had turned it in, Higgins said, "It's not suitable."

Rachel's heart fell. "I thought it was pretty good," she said.

Higgins kept a straight face and said, "That's the trouble. It's more than pretty good. This is such a beautiful piece of writing, so poetic, colorful, and *graphic* in its descriptions of the sea that it makes the stories you are introducing seem very dull by comparison."

He went on a bit later, "I think what you've written is a piece of literature." He urged her to keep it as her own property. He told her to write a simpler introduction for the booklet.

"What will I do with this piece of literature, as you call it?" she asked.

"Send it to a magazine. Somebody will pay money for it," Higgins replied.

"Oh, my, do you really think so? Which magazine?"

"I'm sure someone will want it. Why not start at the top? Send it to the *Atlantic Monthly.*"

Rachel was too modest. She put the manuscript away and turned to other matters.

At last, in 1936, she began to sell some short articles to the *Baltimore Sun*. She wrote articles about fishing, but the articles were different from ordinary sports stories. She explained that bad fishing methods and pollution were killing commercial fishing. Rachel received little money for these occasional articles. But they did give her a feeling of confidence about her writing.

Then in 1937 she remembered Higgins's advice. She sent the original article to the *Atlantic Monthly*. It was accepted. She received $75, a good price in those days.

Her friend Higgins was delighted. "Well, you're going to write a book now, aren't you?"

"I've always wanted to, but . . .," she said.

Higgins suggested that she take the article and break it into little pieces. Each section would make a delightful chapter. The book would be a plea for proper use of our sea resources—marine ecology.

A famous writer, Hendrik Willem van Loon, read the magazine article by R. L. Carson. Rachel had used her initials. She thought an article by a woman might not be taken seriously. Van Loon urged his publisher, Simon and Schuster, to publish a book by this new writer.

At last, after much letter writing and work, Rachel completed the book. She called it *Under the Sea Wind.* It was soundly based in science, but it read like an exciting novel. It was published on November 6, 1941, and received good reviews. A month later came Pearl Harbor. World War II had reached the United States. All thoughts were directed toward the war. Rachel's book sold only 5,000 copies and was soon forgotten.

In her first three years on the job, Rachel was promoted three times. Male employees went off to war, and Rachel became more and more important in the office. She prepared a government pamphlet for the war effort. She sadly noticed that the war effort was seriously damaging the environment. Plains, forest, rivers, and seacoasts were all affected. After the war, the damage went on. America was careless about its precious environment.

Rachel began to prepare booklets on wildlife conservation. She helped found many bird and animal *refuges,* places where these creatures could be protected. Her professional career was bright. She became editor in chief of the Information Division of the Fish and Wildlife Service. She worked closely with Bob Hines, a wildlife artist.

Her first book had not been a financial success, but she kept her hopes up. She got an agent, Marie Rodell, and continued to gather material for another book. This would be a work on oceanography, the study of the ocean environment.

She took a leave of absence in 1949 to write the book. Her 81-year-old mother did the typing. The book was called *The Sea Around Us.* It was published on July 2, 1951, and became a world success. Carson won many awards for it. A film based on it won an Oscar.

The success of this second book gave someone a good idea. Why not publish the first book again? *Under the Sea Wind* had failed because of the war. Perhaps it deserved a second chance. It was published again in 1952. It succeeded this time. Rachel had two books on the bestseller list!

Her writing now took up most of her time. She resigned from the Fish and Wildlife Service. Her third book, *The Edge of the Sea,* dealt with the life at tide line.

In 1958 Rachel received a letter that changed her life. A close friend, Olga Owens Huckins, wrote about careless insect spraying in her neighborhood. Many birds were killed by the masses of DDT on the ground, in birdbaths, and in the bodies of insects. Rachel had planned a book about the earth in ages past. She changed her mind. She saw now that her job was to awaken the American public to the dangers of pollution.

She devoted the next years to government studies about wildlife. Many pamphlets showed the harmful effects of pollution. Careless spraying of chemicals killed fish, birds, and other wildlife. The situation was desperate, but the public knew little about it.

During this period of hard work, Rachel discovered that she had cancer. She kept on. She finished a new edition of *The Sea Around Us*. In the introduction to the new edition, she warned about the dangers of polluting the oceans. Who knew what effect these substances might have on the world of the future?

Then she gave special attention to pesticides. These chemicals used for killing insects had done a lot of good. But their careless, heedless use was doing a lot of harm. She called for intelligent use of pesticides and control of those who use them. She especially attacked DDT. It doesn't disappear. It goes from insect to fish to human being or from fish to bird to human being. She pointed out that there are safer ways to control many pests. Some bacteria, for example, kill certain pests and leave other living things alone.

Her book *Silent Spring* was published in 1962. Its title suggests a possible future world. If we upset nature's balance, the birds will be gone. Bees will die out. Flowers will not be pollinated. The entire chain of being will be in danger. All life will end.

"Watch out! Take care! Look ahead!" The book made its point.

The book was both attacked and praised. Chemical

manufacturers criticized Rachel's conclusions. They pointed out that chemistry had helped human beings in their fight against insect pests. The manufacturers had to agree, however, that her facts were generally correct.

Most voices were favorable. Magazines, newspapers, and television took up her cry. Rachel was showered with honors and awards. She was asked to speak at many important gatherings.

On June 4, 1963, she spoke to a Senate committee. The 125 seats were filled with people who wanted to hear and see her. Senator Abraham Ribicoff of Connecticut said, "Miss Carson, on behalf of the committee, we certainly welcome you here. You are the lady who started all this. . . . There is no doubt in the mind of any American today that we are dealing with a very serious and complicated problem."

The senator continued: "I think that all the people in this country and around the world owe you a debt of gratitude for your writings and your actions toward making the atmosphere and the environment safe. . . . We welcome you here."

This was the beginning of the battle for environmental protection. People were aroused. Members of Congress listened to their *constituents,* the people whom they represent in Washington. Stricter laws began to be passed. But the way was long, and the problem will never be completely solved.

Meanwhile the cancer was weakening Rachel. On April 14, 1964, she died. She had struggled to the end for the cause she believed in—saving the environment.

UNDERSTANDING WHAT YOU HAVE READ

Finding Another Title

1. Another good title for this selection might be **(a)** Rachel Carson and the Fight for the Environment **(b)** Why Pollution Affects Everyone **(c)** The Story of a Writer and the Sea **(d)** Rachel Carson's Abilities as a Writer.

Getting the Main Idea

2. The key sentence in this chapter is
   (a) Rachel was very much interested in English, especially writing.
   (b) The Great Depression began.
   (c) Her writing now took up most of her time.
   (d) Every living thing exists in relation to its environment and to other living things.

Finding Details

3. All the following natural disasters are mentioned EXCEPT **(a)** hurricanes **(b)** drought **(c)** blizzards **(d)** earthquakes.

4. One unfortunate side effect of DDT was that **(a)** it was bitter to the taste **(b)** it showed up in the bodies of living things **(c)** it killed only one insect in ten **(d)** it became too expensive to buy.

5. The most important influence on Rachel Carson's life was **(a)** Professor C. J. Pierpont **(b)** Dr. Raymond Pearl **(c)** Elmer Higgins **(d)** Senator Abraham Ribicoff.

6. She was first paid for articles printed in **(a)** the *Atlantic Monthly* **(b)** the *Baltimore Sun* **(c)** a college magazine **(d)** the *National Geographic*.

7. Hendrik Willem van Loon was (a) a biologist (b) a senator (c) an editor (d) a writer.
8. The book that failed on its first appearance was (a) *The Sea Around Us* (b) *Silent Spring* (c) *Under the Sea Wind* (d) *The Edge of the Sea.*
9. The letter that changed Rachel Carson's life and led her to write *Silent Spring* was from (a) a close friend (b) her mother (c) her father (d) her teacher.
10. Her appearance before the Senate committee took place in (a) 1937 (b) 1941 (c) 1958 (d) 1963.

Making Inferences

11. Rachel Carson's childhood experiences with nature (a) influenced her life's work (b) were unhappy (c) aroused her interest in mechanical objects (d) did not prepare her for later life.
12. The episode about the goat is introduced to (a) add a little humor (b) show Rachel's scientific interests (c) explain the rivalry between the Army and the Navy (d) trace Rachel's love of animals.
13. When Higgins told Rachel that her introduction was unsuitable, he was (a) a little cruel (b) angry (c) teasing her (d) completely incorrect.
14. Rachel Carson was special because she (a) was able to illustrate her own books (b) refused to speak in public (c) was both a skilled writer and a good scientist (d) never had to change a single opinion in her life.
15. Pesticides (a) should never be used (b) should be used carefully and not too often (c) are always harmful (d) were stopped immediately after *Silent Spring* was published.

Predicting What Happens Next

16. After Rachel Carson's death (a) her books were no longer read (b) she was given a military medal of honor (c) experts showed how wrong she had been (d) others took up the fight she had begun.

Deciding on the Order of Events

17. The following events are scrambled. Arrange them in proper order, as they happened. Use letters only.
    (a) Rachel takes a civil service exam and passes.
    (b) Elmer Higgins tells Rachel to write a book.
    (c) Rachel studies at Woods Hole during the summer.
    (d) *Silent Spring* is published.

Inferring Tone

18. Senator Ribicoff's attitude toward Rachel Carson (41) was one of (a) irritation (b) curiosity (c) worry (d) respect.

Separating Facts from Opinions

For each of the following, tell whether the statement is a fact (*F*) or an opinion (*O*).
19. Rachel Carson attended Johns Hopkins University.
20. Rachel Carson is the most effective science writer of all time.

Understanding Words from Context

21. We have moved in the right direction and made great *strides* in protecting the environment.
    Strides (35) means (a) long steps (b) decisions (c) mistakes (d) films.

22. The goat is a symbol of the Navy team and is supposed to bring it good fortune. Someone suggested getting a goat as a *mascot* for Rachel's team.
A *mascot* (36) is supposed to   (a) play on a team   (b) be a friend   (c) manage a team   (d) bring good luck.

23. "This is such a beautiful piece of writing, so poetic, colorful, and *graphic* in its descriptions of the sea that it makes the stories you are introducing seem very dull by comparison."
Graphic (37) means   (a) sad   (b) vivid   (c) uninteresting   (d) wordy.

24. She helped found many bird and animal *refuges,* places where these creatures could be protected.
Refuges (39) are   (a) traps   (b) escapes   (c) safe places   (d) strong cages.

25. Members of Congress listened to their *constituents,* the people whom they represent.
Constituents (41) are   (a) voters in a district   (b) naturalized citizens   (c) legal assistants   (d) friends in Washington.

THINKING IT OVER

1. What do you think would have happened if Rachel Carson had not sounded the alarm about pollution?
2. Few successful lives have been easy. What problems did Rachel Carson face in her career?
3. Why did *Under the Sea Wind* fail the first time? Does luck play a part in success? Can you provide examples to prove your point?
4. Margaret Mead studied the behavior of human beings in different cultures. She once wrote, "We

are living beyond our means." What do you think she meant? Do you agree? Why or why not?

5. What other examples can you think of to show that one person can make a great difference?

6. Should pesticides be banned altogether? What problems would a total ban bring? What might be the best solution?

7. What recent examples of environmental pollution have you read about or heard about? Could something have been done to prevent the harm?

8. Many polluting materials are suspected of causing cancer. Rachel Carson died of cancer. Might Carson herself have been a victim of such pollution? Or was it just a coincidence? What do you think?

9. What part do the oceans play in helping living things?

10. What quality in Rachel Carson do you most admire? Why?

ANOTHER LOOK AT THE QUOTATION

> *I truly believe that the fundamental*
> *[basic] principles of ecology govern our*
> *lives, wherever we live, and that we*
> *must wake up to this fact or be lost.*
> KARIN SHELDON

1. Explain the quotation in your own words.
2. How do we depend upon the environment for our very lives?
3. Has the quality of your environment been affected recently? Tell about it.
4. In small villages in Europe the church bell was rung to announce the death of a villager. In a famous sermon, the preacher and poet John Donne

once said, "Never send to know for whom the bell tolls. It tolls for thee." What did he mean? Would Rachel Carson have agreed with him? Why or why not?

WORDS AT YOUR SERVICE—SYNONYMS

> *Many insects developed* immunity *to DDT. Some individual insects were not killed by it. (34)*

Notice how the two sentences tell you all you need to know to figure out the meaning of *immunity*. An insect with immunity to a chemical *cannot be killed* by it. The chemical has no effect on the insect.

The paired sentences gave you the clue to the meaning of *immunity*. Often a single sentence provides clues to the meaning of a word within the sentence. Study the following sentence:

> *The valley of the Allegheny River was heavily polluted, and the river itself was* foul.

Notice that the word *polluted* is tied to the word *foul*. If the word *foul* is new to you, the pairing of *polluted* and *foul* should help with the meaning.

Synonyms are words with roughly the same meaning. *Polluted* and *foul* are synonyms. Sometimes synonyms are directly paired in a sentence. This kind of wording gives you a clear clue to the meaning of an unfamiliar word in the pair. Here's another sentence from the selection:

> *But their careless,* heedless *use was doing a lot of harm.*

Here *careless* and *heedless* are paired. They are synonyms. You probably already know the meaning of *careless*. If *heedless* is new to you, you now know that it means something like *careless*.

Study the following sentences and then guess at the meaning of each *italicized* word. Use your understanding of synonyms to help you.

EXAMPLE

Anna's solution to the problem was too *involved,* too complicated for me to follow.

Involved means **(a)** crystal clear **(b)** funny **(c)** difficult **(d)** unexpected.

Since *involved* is linked with *complicated,* the answer is **(c)** *difficult.*

1. The Vietnam Memorial is a lasting, *enduring* tribute to those Americans who gave their lives in the Vietnam War.

   Enduring means **(a)** meaningful **(b)** attractive **(c)** permanent **(d)** sad.

2. I often *crave* pizza and long for it most often just before bedtime.

   Crave means **(a)** bake **(b)** talk about **(c)** give up **(d)** desire.

3. An approaching tornado is a scary, *fearsome* sight.

   Fearsome means **(a)** brightly lit **(b)** frightening **(c)** pleasant **(d)** wet.

4. The noise from the construction gradually *diminished,* becoming less and less as time passed.

   Diminished means **(a)** lessened **(b)** increased **(c)** became more pleasant **(d)** stopped altogether.

5. We laughed at Bill's *quip,* his witty remark about the way our team played our last game.

   A *quip* is a **(a)** joke **(b)** sad statement **(c)** reading from a magazine **(d)** kind of encouragement.

DANIEL HALE WILLIAMS:

Pioneer Heart Surgeon

The best way out is always through.
ROBERT FROST

Cape Town, South Africa, made headlines in December 1967 when Dr. Christiaan Barnard successfully transplanted a heart from one person to another. A young woman had been killed in an automobile accident. Her heart was transferred to the body of a man. While the operation itself was a success, the man died of pneumonia 18 days later.

A month later Dr. Barnard performed another heart-transplant operation. In the months that followed, more and more people received the hearts of others. The operation itself is a most difficult and scary one. But the real problem comes after the operation.

Our bodies have all kinds of self-defense *mechanisms*. One of these devices works to reject foreign substances. The body has no way of knowing that a new heart is a lifesaving organ. It sets up all kinds of reactions to get rid of the foreign heart.

Doctors have learned more and more how to *cope* with this most dangerous problem. Heart-transplant operations have become more and more successful. Today heart-transplant patients can expect to live fairly normal lives.

In some patients, for one reason or another, a human heart cannot be transplanted. In such cases some doctors have recommended using an artificial heart.

Even before the first heart transplant, doctors had experimented with artificial devices to keep the heart beating. On April 21, 1966, Dr. Michael De Bakey of Houston, Texas, *implanted* a heart pump in a patient. Mrs. Esperanza del Valle of Mexico City survived the operation and returned home within a month. Nowadays pacemakers are routinely implanted in human hearts, but in 1966, mechanical devices to assist the heart were still experimental.

In 1966 De Bakey believed that a device to replace the

human heart was far in the future. Just 16 years later, in 1982, surgeons put a completely artificial heart in the body of Barney Clark. The Jarvik heart, named after its inventor, is able to do its job. It requires a lot of machinery to keep it running. It does the job well, but the body doesn't welcome this outside organ either. Clark lived for only 112 days after the operation.

Some doctors see the mechanical heart as a temporary step until a transplant can be found. Others point out that there are never enough transplant hearts available. About one-third of the patients who need a transplant die before a heart can be found. Keeping the most hopeless patients alive makes the shortage of available hearts worse. Some of these people, doctors say, may be more likely to die even after transplants. Others with a better chance may not get a needed heart.

The replacement of the heart and other organs has raised many new questions. There was a time, though, when such problems never arose. Doctors could not treat heart disease effectively. Heart surgery was not *obtainable*. It had not yet been tried.

It took one skillful, courageous doctor to lead the way to modern heart surgery. His name was Daniel Hale Williams. This is his story.

The cities in summer can be hot. People become irritable. Even a small disagreement can turn into a fight. Such a fight once helped to make medical history.

It began on a particularly hot day in Chicago in July 1893. James Cornish, a young worker, suffered a knife wound in a fight. He was rushed to Provident Hospital, but the wound didn't seem too serious. Everyone thought that James would soon be released, but they were wrong.

The young man began to weaken. He suffered pains around the heart. He showed all the signs of shock. His condition soon began to look very serious indeed.

Dr. Daniel Hale Williams was called in. Dr. Williams, founder of Provident Hospital, already had a fine name. He was an excellent doctor. As a surgeon, he had already operated successfully hundreds of times. Once, he had performed a successful operation in a dining room when the patient refused to go to the hospital! His warmth, kindness, and consideration for others had earned him the affectionate name "Dr. Dan."

This time Dr. Dan was not hopeful as he looked at the young worker. Perhaps Cornish's heart had been injured. If so, there seemed to be little hope for the wounded man. Remember the date: 1893. Surgery was not the advanced science it is today. Most modern aids had not been invented. There was no X-ray machine. There were fewer surgical instruments. Heart surgery was unknown.

"Leave heart-wound cases alone," the medical books advised young doctors. Doctors tried to keep patients comfortable, but they could do little to help them. As a result, many patients with heart injuries died.

Dr. Dan was not willing to give up so easily. He wanted to try to save the wounded man's life, but it was difficult to know how to do this. For years many important doctors had been saying that heart surgery was impossible. All the experts were against taking chances with the most important organ of the human body, the heart.

Dr. Dan might have said to himself: "If I do nothing, the man will probably die. No one will blame me. I would then have done everything possible for him, in the eyes of my fellow doctors. On the other hand, if I try surgery, the man may die anyway. But then I'll be blamed for his death. The man's chances are not good either way."

Most people do not have to face this kind of life-or-death decision. And few people would want to take the blame for another person's death. But Dr. Dan was no ordinary person and no ordinary doctor. He looked down at the dying man. He listened to the man's coughing and suddenly decided to take the chance. "I'll operate," he said.

There were many problems to face. Cutting into the chest cavity was a dangerous task. Opening the heart area was a terrible thing to consider. Remember that Dr. Dan did not have the help of modern science.

In this history-making operation Dr. Dan had no doctor trained in anesthetics beside him. Anesthetics are the painkillers so *essential* in today's operations; without them, many of today's operations could not be done. He had, of course, no X-ray machine. He did not have a rubber tube to keep the windpipe open. He could not use blood transfusions. And of course he did not have the modern drugs that combat infection. Comparing his equipment with modern medical equipment is like comparing a horse-drawn carriage with a jet airplane.

Dr. Dan was a pioneer. Since no one before him had performed this operation, he had no one to give him advice. As he worked his way through the blood vessels and arteries, he would be all alone. He had to work close to the heart, but he could not interrupt its work. There was the danger, too, that Cornish's lung might collapse when air rushed into the chest cavity. What a tense moment it was when he began to operate!

As Dr. Dan cut into the chest, he soon discovered that an important artery had been damaged. Arteries carry the life-giving blood to various parts of the body. Damage to an artery is serious. Dr. Dan repaired the damage. Then he worked around the heart itself.

Naturally the heart was beating while Dr. Dan worked. Operating was like trying to read a book while riding on a bumpy road. Dr. Dan had to give the job his full attention. He had to use every ounce of his skill. The knife wound had slightly penetrated the heart. If the wound had been a half-inch in any other direction, James Cornish would have died before reaching the hospital. Even a slight *incision* in the area of the heart seemed like a dangerous and deep gash.

The heart itself did not need mending, but the sac, or bag, that encloses the heart had to be sewed. While the tissues were moving with every heartbeat, Dr. Dan began to stitch the wound. It was a moment of great tension. A number of doctors watched as Dr. Dan used his skillful fingers to do the job. Every one had his own thoughts, but everyone wondered, "What if he should fail!"

Dr. Dan didn't fail. He cleansed the wound, sewed it, and closed the chest cavity. Only then did he permit himself to rest. He had successfully performed the first operation on the human heart, but the danger was not over. Would James Cornish ever be able to leave the hospital? Would he develop an infection that would kill him? Would the heart show damage after surgery? Only time would tell.

The first results were discouraging. James Cornish became weaker. His fever rose. He suffered more pain. His pulse rate increased. He had difficulty sleeping. He had trouble breathing. During these tense days Dr. Dan stayed with his patient.

On the third day there was an improvement. On the fourth day the temperature dropped. But on the seventh day there was pain again. The patient had fluid in his lung cavity. Dr. Dan would have to operate again, but he would have to wait. The patient had to get stronger.

Three weeks later Dr. Dan operated again and removed the fluid. Otherwise James was in surprisingly good condition. He began to improve steadily. On August 30, the case was closed. James Cornish had won his battle. Twenty years later he was still alive and in good condition. The world's first heart operation had been a success.

News spread. Others congratulated Dr. Dan. They marveled at his courage and his skill. The hospital became world-famous. Dr. Dan was always known afterward as the first man to "sew up the heart."

Dr. Dan performed at least two similar operations later. One man lived for fifty years after the operation.

In nearly a century much has happened. There has been much progress in heart surgery. But in his own day, Dr. Dan's achievement was great. A black man who rose to the top of his profession and became an outstanding surgeon, Dr. Dan has a secure place in history.

UNDERSTANDING WHAT YOU HAVE READ

Finding Another Title

1. Another good title for this selection might be **(a)** A Difficult Job **(b)** Heart Transplants **(c)** The Story of the Artificial Heart **(d)** Dr. Dan and the First Successful Heart Operation.

Getting the Main Idea

2. Daniel Hale Williams was **(a)** the founder of a hospital **(b)** a pioneer in medicine **(c)** a kind man **(d)** unsuccessful.

Finding Details

3. The first heart transplant was performed by **(a)** Daniel Hale Williams **(b)** Michael De Bakey **(c)** Christiaan Barnard **(d)** Barney Clark.

4. James Cornish suffered from a **(a)** weak heart **(b)** knife wound **(c)** childhood disease **(d)** nervous breakdown.
5. The founder of Provident Hospital was **(a)** Daniel Hale Williams **(b)** James Cornish **(c)** Michael De Bakey **(d)** someone else, whose name was not mentioned.
6. Before Dr. Dan's attempt, heart operations were considered **(a)** too risky **(b)** useful by most doctors **(c)** interesting but unimportant **(d)** common.
7. Dr. Dan had the following equipment for his operation: **(a)** rubber tube **(b)** thread **(c)** modern drugs **(d)** modern anesthetics.
8. When Dr. Dan began to operate, he discovered damage to **(a)** an artery **(b)** a vein **(c)** the liver **(d)** the throat.
9. The heart is enclosed in a kind of bag called **(a)** tissues **(b)** the lung cavity **(c)** a sac **(d)** fluid.
10. The man who lived for fifty years after the operation was **(a)** Dr. Christiaan Barnard **(b)** James Cornish **(c)** Daniel Williams **(d)** not named.

Making Inferences

11. In Dr. Dan's time heart operations were not tried because the heart seemed so **(a)** strong anyway **(b)** unimportant to most surgeons **(c)** difficult to work with **(d)** easily helped by rest.
12. The comparison of a jet airplane and a horse-drawn carriage points out **(a)** differences **(b)** similarities **(c)** communication **(d)** transportation.
13. In his operation Dr. Dan was very **(a)** humorous **(b)** afraid **(c)** careful **(d)** clumsy.

14. In the position of his wound and in his treatment by Dr. Dan, James Cornish was certainly **(a)** unlucky **(b)** lucky **(c)** strong **(d)** gentle.

15. When James Cornish became weaker after the operation, Dr. Dan probably **(a)** left on a trip **(b)** called in a heart doctor from Boston **(c)** gave up hope **(d)** became worried.

Predicting What Happens Next

16. After the operation other doctors probably **(a)** became interested in how Dr. Dan worked **(b)** did not believe Dr. Dan **(c)** replaced Dr. Dan within a year **(d)** brought James Cornish to New York to study his case.

Deciding on the Order of Events

17. The following events are scrambled. Arrange them in proper order, as they happened. Use letters only.
(a) Dr. Barnard completes the first heart transplant.
(b) Dr. Dan operates on a wounded worker.
(c) Barney Clark receives an artificial heart.
(d) James Cornish survives the first open-heart surgery.

Inferring Tone

18. When Dr. Dan said, "I'll operate" (53), his tone was **(a)** frightened **(b)** tired **(c)** light and cheerful **(d)** firm.

Separating Facts from Opinions

For each of the following, tell whether the statement is a fact (*F*) or an opinion (*O*).

19. Replacing a human heart with an artificial heart is a bad idea.
20. Daniel Hale Williams should not have operated on James Cornish.

Understanding Words from Context

21. Our bodies have all kinds of self-defense *mechanisms*. One of these responses is to reject foreign substances.
   Mechanisms (50) means **(a)** devices **(b)** hearts **(c)** ways of thinking **(d)** opportunities.
22. Doctors have learned more and more how to *cope* with this most dangerous problem. Heart-transplant operations have become more and more successful.
   Cope (50) means **(a)** play **(b)** suffer **(c)** deal **(d)** surrender.
23. On April 21, 1966, Dr. Michael De Bakey of Houston, Texas, *implanted* a heart pump in a patient.
   Implanted (50) means **(a)** discovered **(b)** placed **(c)** removed **(d)** described.
24. Heart surgery was not *obtainable*. It had not yet been tried.
   Obtainable (51) means **(a)** can be gotten **(b)** not easily available **(c)** safe or easy to use **(d)** openly discussed.
25. Anesthetics are the painkillers so *essential* in today's operations; without them, many of today's operations could not be done.
   Essential (53) means **(a)** poorly handled **(b)** lacking **(c)** seldom used **(d)** necessary.

THINKING IT OVER

1. Why did Dr. Dan decide to perform heart surgery?
2. What made heart surgery so difficult in those days?
3. Why is it so difficult to be the first in anything? Were you ever the first to do or try something? Tell about your experience.
4. Why are most people willing to follow the crowd? When is it necessary *not* to follow the crowd?
5. What other examples of great surgery have you heard or read about?
6. What other examples of scientific or medical advances can you think of?
7. Sometimes scientific gains bring on new problems, like pollution. What other examples of problems can you suggest?

ANOTHER LOOK AT THE QUOTATION

The best way out is always through.
ROBERT FROST

1. Though this is one of the shortest quotations in this book, it is one of the deepest. What does Robert Frost mean?
2. Have you solved problems by working at them directly, or have you avoided them? Which method does Frost approve of?
3. Did Daniel Hale Williams follow Frost's advice in solving the heart-surgery problem? Explain.

WORDS AT YOUR SERVICE—COMPARISONS

> *Even a slight* incision *in the area of the heart seemed like a dangerous and deep gash. (54)*

If *incision* is a new word for you, notice that you have help with its meaning. Since it is being compared with a *deep gash,* it must mean a *cut.*

If you hear someone called "as *skittish* as a colt in a thunderstorm," you can guess that *skittish* means *easily frightened.* Suppose you hear someone say, "That cat *stalks* a mouse like a lion creeping up on an antelope." The comparison tells you that *stalk* means *approach silently.*

Study the following sentences and then guess at the meaning of each *italicized* word. Use the comparison in the sentence to help you.

EXAMPLE

When he is angry, Stan holds himself as *rigid* as a bar of metal.

Rigid means   **(a)** quiet   **(b)** loose   **(c)** stiff   **(d)** polite.

Since a bar of metal is stiff and firm, the correct answer is **(c)** *stiff.*

1. Like pirates aboard a merchant vessel, the thieves *ransacked* the room, looking for jewelry and money.
   Ransacked means   **(a)** lit up   **(b)** gently entered   **(c)** neatly examined   **(d)** searched furiously.

2. The children *frolicked* like kittens on the well-kept lawn.
   Frolicked means   **(a)** played   **(b)** argued   **(c)** fought bitterly   **(d)** sat quietly.

3. The streets of the city were *teeming* with people looking like ants around a large anthill.
Teeming means **(a)** motionless **(b)** chilly **(c)** crowded **(d)** gleaming.

4. The fictional detective was as *oblivious* to danger as a moth around a flame.
Oblivious means **(a)** afraid **(b)** certain **(c)** unaware of **(d)** weary.

5. If Max is disturbed at sleep, he shows all the *irritability* of an angry wasp.
Irritability means **(a)** sweetness **(b)** bad temper **(c)** sense of wonder **(d)** many colors.

ANOTHER LOOK

HOW MUCH DO YOU REMEMBER?

1. The person who was a close friend of Isaac Newton is **(a)** Charles Babbage **(b)** Jack Kilby **(c)** Edmund Halley **(d)** Maria Carson.

2. The person who was a doctor of medicine is **(a)** Rachel Carson **(b)** Daniel Hale Williams **(c)** Robert Noyce **(d)** Lady Ada Lovelace.

3. The danger of careless use of chemicals was pointed out by **(a)** C. J. Pierpont **(b)** Charles Babbage **(c)** Daniel Hale Williams **(d)** Rachel Carson.

4. The person who became famous as a writer is **(a)** Charles Babbage **(b)** James Cornish **(c)** Rachel Carson **(d)** Harold, the king of England.

5. Two names that are linked together are **(a)** Mark Twain and Edmund Halley **(b)** Charles Babbage and Elmer Higgins **(c)** Edmund Halley and Daniel Hale Williams **(d)** Isaac Newton and Robert Noyce.

6. The person who died with his work not completed is **(a)** Charles Babbage **(b)** Edmund Halley **(c)** Daniel Hale Williams **(d)** Jack Kilby.

7. At one time comets were thought to **(a)** bring on a period of good times **(b)** come from the moon **(c)** come from the sun **(d)** warn of troubles ahead.

8. Compared with modern computers, Babbage's calculating machine is (**a**) more beautiful (**b**) much larger (**c**) easier to use (**d**) more suited for certain kinds of work.
9. The book *Silent Spring* warns of (**a**) a world severely damaged by pollution (**b**) the danger of nuclear explosions (**c**) the rapid exhaustion of our energy resources (**d**) the failure of the schools to teach reading.
10. Isaac Newton is famous for his (**a**) exploration of the South Seas (**b**) theory about calculating machines (**c**) theory of gravitation (**d**) invention of the microscope.

WHAT IS YOUR OPINION?

1. Which person in this unit seems to you to have done the most for humanity? Defend your choice.
2. In what way was each of the four people in this unit a true pioneer?
3. Greatness doesn't allow discouragement. How did each of the people in this unit attack discouragement?
4. What are some recent scientific discoveries that seem very important?
5. If you had a chance to become a great doctor or a famous astronomer, which would you choose? Why?
6. A robot is a computerized mechanical person. What movies have you seen about robots? Were the robots made to seem friendly or dangerous? Tell about them.

THE QUOTATION AND THE UNIT

> *Genius has the power of lighting its*
> *own fire.*
>
> JOHN FOSTER

1. Explain the quotation in your own words.
2. How did each of the subjects in this unit light his or her own fire?
3. Geniuses have to be stubborn in following their own dreams. Can stubbornness sometimes be wrong? Explain.
4. What is the difference between talent and genius?

UNIT 2

THE STAGE AND THE ARENA

If you play it safe in life, you've decided that you don't want to grow anymore.
SHIRLEY HUFSTEDLER

Of all recreations, sports and acting are especially popular. People like to watch and to take part. People enjoy playing tennis, golf, and other sports activities. They also enjoy taking part in amateur performances of plays and musicals.

This unit selects three subjects from the stage and two from the sports arena. All five had to struggle to succeed, but all also won great success.

For a hundred years the operettas of Gilbert and Sullivan have been highly popular.

65

Though the first of their operettas was not a success, they tried again. Each new operetta seemed more popular than the one before. At this very moment one of their operettas is probably being played somewhere.

Debbie Allen is a modern representative of the stage. Unlike Gilbert and Sullivan, she is a performer. She has had experience on the stage, in the movies, and on television. In just a few years she has reached the top of her profession.

Martina Navratilova and Kareem Abdul-Jabbar were blessed by nature with magnificent bodies. They have the strength, the talent, and the skill to win. But more important, they have the will to win. Each one is a champion. Each one had to rise above defeat and show the world true courage. In tennis and in basketball there are only a few truly great athletes. Martina and Kareem are among these.

All the people in this unit have delighted audiences and spectators the world over. All five have given new glory to the stage or the sports arena.

W. S. GILBERT AND ARTHUR SULLIVAN:
Masters of the Comic Opera

If you approach each new person you meet in a spirit of adventure, you will find yourself endlessly fascinated by the new channels of thought and experience and personality that you encounter.
ELEANOR ROOSEVELT

At a very early age, Frederic was apprenticed to pirates. An apprentice is someone who learns a trade while working on the job. As an apprentice, he learned the trade well, but he was unhappy. Frederic was not a pirate at heart. Still he was a slave to duty. He knew that his period as apprentice would end on his twenty-first birthday.

On that birthday he left his former mates and became respectable. A few days later the Pirate King realized that since Frederic had been born on February 29, Leap Year Day, he really had a birthday only once every four years. So instead of being 21, Frederic was just a little more than five! As a slave to duty, Frederic had to rejoin the pirates.

This incident forms the heart of the plot of *The Pirates of Penzance* by Gilbert and Sullivan. But there are many other upside-down incidents in this comic opera. For example, the reason Frederic was apprenticed to a pirate was that his nursemaid had misunderstood his father's instructions. She thought he had said *pirate,* but he really had said *pilot.*

More than a hundred years have passed since the first production of *The Pirates of Penzance,* but it is as popular as ever. A production is the show produced on the stage. A recent movie of it with Linda Ronstadt and Kevin Kline appeared in theaters and on television. In addition, *The Pirates of Penzance* and ten other Gilbert and Sullivan operettas appeared on public television. All over the world amateur and professional groups put on Gilbert and Sullivan productions.

Why should operettas, or light operas, of another day continue to be produced and enjoyed? After all, many of the situations are out of date. Many of the real-life people mentioned in the plays have been long forgotten. The music itself is of another time. At least, you might think the operettas dated. That is, until you see a production. Probably not a day passes without a Gilbert and Sullivan operetta produced somewhere in the world. Why? We can list several reasons, but no explanation can capture what is special about these little gems. Of the 14 Gilbert and Sullivan operettas, 11 are still regularly played. All the operettas have comical, topsy-turvy plots. In *H.M.S. Pinafore,* for example, the captain and a humble seaman were switched in their cradles, when they were babies. Thus the person who should have become the captain has become the lowly sailor, and vice versa. In *The Mikado,* the Lord High Executioner, a comical figure, has to execute someone to show he is doing his job. But the person to be executed is the Mikado's son, who has been in disguise. Of course, all the confusions are cleared up in the end. Meanwhile they provide a lot of fun.

There are two major reasons for the success of Gilbert and Sullivan. These are Gilbert's words and Sullivan's music. Both are exceptional. Each man contributes a special skill.

Gilbert's words are brilliant. The talk between characters is skillful and appealing. Gilbert's lines make the characters come to life. He includes *patter songs* in the operas. These are comical, witty verses sung at rapid speed with remarkably clever words. They always leave the audience asking for more.

Sullivan's music is lovely. It is always right for the action. It often pokes fun at serious music. In doing so, it creates beautiful music of its own. When Gilbert's words are matched with Sullivan's music, the results are magical. People leave the theater humming the music and singing some of the lyrics.

Partnerships are always difficult. To work closely together, people must learn to control their tempers. They must learn to be careful in presenting their points of view. They must consider their own success less important than the success of the partnership, or *collaboration,* as it is sometimes called. They must be strong individuals, yet able to give in at times.

For more than 25 years Gilbert and Sullivan worked together. For such a long partnership you would expect the two people to be somewhat alike. In their case, nothing could be further from the truth. Gilbert and Sullivan were opposites. That they got together in the first place was surprising. That they worked successfully together for a long time was a miracle. They had bitter differences at times. But for the most part, they managed to control their irritations.

William Schwenck Gilbert was born on November 18, 1836, in London. His father was a former naval surgeon. At age 25, the father inherited enough money to retire. He was a strong-minded individual, and his son shared many of those traits.

At the age of two, young Gilbert was taken to Naples, Italy, on a holiday with his parents. While there he was kidnapped and held briefly for ransom. The ransom of 25 pounds (British dollars) was paid, and young William seemed none the worse for his experience. He remembered the kidnapping all his life, though, and used it as a basis for the plots of several operettas.

At 13, the young man was sent to Great Ealing School. He stood out as a clever boy. He won several prizes for being a good student. Within three years he was the head boy of the school, but he was not popular. He was too sure of himself. He easily became angry. He had no patience with anyone less brilliant then he. These character traits stayed with him all his life.

He had a government job at one time—and hated it. He became a soldier for a while. As a soldier and as a government clerk, he loved practical jokes. His sense of fun kept him from becoming too bored.

Like his father, he also inherited money. He immediately left government service and decided to become a lawyer. He wasn't very successful, though. In his first two years as a lawyer, he earned only about 75 pounds ($375) a year. But he was gaining all kinds of experiences. Indeed, his life as a government clerk, a soldier, and a lawyer gave him ideas for later writing.

William decided to try his hand at writing. Like most beginning writers, he tasted failure. Editors returned article after article. Then he had his first lucky break. He was invited to write a weekly column for the magazine *Fun*. He also supplied a drawing for each column. He had a talent for comic art as well as for writing.

In the following years Gilbert became well known as a writer of comic verse, plays, and stories. He wrote a series of poems called *The Bab Ballads*. Many of these supplied material for later operettas.

If nothing further had happened, Gilbert would probably now be forgotten. Some scholars would read his poems and stories, but few would know his name. Then a special event occurred. Gilbert and Sullivan were invited to create an operetta. In 1871 Gilbert and Sullivan's *Thespis* appeared on the Gaiety Theater program.

Arthur Sullivan was six years younger than Gilbert. He was born in London on May 13, 1842. His father was a poorly paid professional musician. His mother had to leave Arthur with a babysitter so that she could go out to work as a teacher in a family with children.

Shortly after, however, the Sullivans' fortunes improved. Arthur's father was appointed bandmaster at the Sandhurst Military College. Young Arthur loved to listen to the bands practice. Once in a while he was allowed to play an instrument.

Arthur's interest in music grew with the years. He joined a group of young singers and was invited to sing many solo parts. As a boy, Arthur loved to compose music. Before he was 13, he had composed an anthem.

When he was 14, Arthur won the Mendelssohn Scholarship for music. A scholarship is a grant of money. He was so talented that he won it for the next two years as well. He was recognized as the outstanding student at the Royal Academy of Music. In 1858 the Scholarship Fund Committee sent him to Germany for further study.

Arthur began composing in earnest. He wrote music for Shakespeare's play *The Tempest*. He wrote his Symphony in E-flat. He composed *In Memoriam,* which was a triumph at a music festival.

All these honors brought him into the company of the famous. He met several members of the royal family, including the Prince of Wales. He was a close friend of the duke of Edinburgh. He met many famous musicians, artists, and writers.

At this time he fell in love with Rachel Russell, daughter of a wealthy Scottish engineer. Unfortunately, Rachel's mother did not approve of him. The relationship dragged on for years. At last, Rachel married someone else and sailed to India with her husband. By then, Sullivan was relieved.

In 1866 Sullivan composed the music for *Cox and Box,* a light opera written by F. C. Burnand. It was a great success. Sullivan and Burnand were *induced* to put on another operetta, but this one played to half-empty theaters. Sullivan was deeply disappointed.

Friends urged Sullivan to try his hand at another comic opera. Sullivan was too discouraged to try again with Burnand. Then in 1871 came a letter inviting him to write the music for something written by W. S. Gilbert. The rest is history.

Gilbert and Sullivan had already met, in 1869. Neither one had particularly liked the other then. Gilbert was a strong-minded, know-it-all type. He was easily enraged. He had no sympathy for people he considered less intelligent than he. He could lose his temper at a moment's notice. He attacked his writing as if he were a general attacking an enemy army. He wrote because he *had to* write.

By contrast, Sullivan was easygoing, mild, sweet-natured. He rarely got angry. He was gentle with all people. He liked to live well and worked with Gilbert because he needed the money to support the life-style he enjoyed.

At their first meeting Gilbert tried to challenge Sullivan's musical knowledge. Sullivan did not take to Gilbert at all. He avoided him and *declined* a suggestion that he might work with Gilbert on an operetta. Then something happened.

A producer named John Hollingshead wrote that letter in 1871 inviting Sullivan to work with Gilbert. For some reason, perhaps because he needed the money, Sullivan agreed to try an operetta with Gilbert.

Their first operetta was called *Thespis*. Working on the operetta was not a good experience. Only a week's rehearsal was allowed. There wasn't time to do a good job. Some of the singers were annoyed by Gilbert's bossy manner.

At one point Nellie Farren, the star of the show, said, "Really, Mr. Gilbert, why should I stand here? I am not a chorus girl."

"No, madam," Gilbert replied, "your voice isn't strong enough, or you would be."

Sullivan agreed with Gilbert, though. He said later, "Among the difficulties was the fact that in those days there were few actors or actresses who could sing."

In later operettas Gilbert and Sullivan developed their own singers.

Thespis was a failure. Of all the Gilbert and Sullivan operettas, this is the only one that was never played again. Some of the words and music were used in later operettas, but *Thespis* died.

With the failure behind them, Gilbert and Sullivan might have ended their partnership. It's surprising that Gilbert and Sullivan ever got together again after *Thespis*. They were both becoming successful on their own. In the three years after *Thespis*, for example, Sullivan wrote 47 hymns, including "Onward, Christian Soldiers." Gilbert was writing successful nonmusical comedies.

The world owes a great debt to Richard D'Oyly Carte. It was he who made the Gilbert and Sullivan operettas possible. He was a keen businessman who saw the possibilities in a partnership. He took over the management of the Royalty Theater. He hoped to make it the home of English comic opera.

Gilbert had written a play, *Trial by Jury*. He had hoped that a friend of his would write the music. The two planned to have the friend's wife star in it. When the wife died, the plan was abandoned. D'Oyly Carte suggested Gilbert bring the idea to Sullivan.

Gilbert hurried over to Sullivan's home and asked if he might read the piece to him. Sullivan agreed. He fidgeted, and Gilbert read faster and faster. Gilbert thought Sullivan disliked the play, but actually Sullivan loved it. They agreed to do *Trial by Jury* together.

The operetta was produced at the Royalty Theater on March 25, 1875. It was a great hit *then*. It is a great hit *still*. The part of the judge was played by Frederic Sullivan, Arthur's brother. A year later Frederic died, and Sullivan wrote "The Lost Chord" in grief. For a while Sullivan had no appetite for composing.

After a time, Sullivan began writing again. He and Gilbert created another operetta, *The Sorcerer,* which opened on November 17, 1877. For this work Gilbert and Sullivan asked for little-known performers. They didn't want big stars who refused to be directed. D'Oyly Carte sided with Gilbert and Sullivan. This decision affected all later plays. Gilbert and Sullivan molded the players to the parts.

Their next operetta, *H.M.S. Pinafore,* was a smash hit. The music was played all over London. The song "Little Buttercup" could be heard in restaurants, music halls, and homes everywhere. Even the words became popular.

At one point in the operetta, the captain sings, "I'm never, never sick at sea!"

The sailors ask, "What, never?"

The captain replies, "No, never!"

Then the sailors ask again, "What, *never?*"

The captain admits, "Hardly ever!"

Soon the words *hardly ever* became part of people's everyday conversation.

Life didn't always run smoothly. Gilbert had many ideas for operettas, but Sullivan often objected to the suggested plots. Sullivan felt that the operettas were beneath him. He wanted to be known for more serious works. He created an opera, *Ivanhoe,* which is almost forgotten today. Though Sullivan was not too eager, he *reluctantly* agreed again and again to work with his difficult partner.

During the work on an operetta, there were often disagreements. Sullivan *resented* Gilbert's manner. Gilbert was bothered by Sullivan's hurt feelings. Yet somehow these two people managed to create musical works that have outlasted most of the serious shows of the time. Theirs was a love-hate relationship, but it worked.

The most important disagreement came over a new

carpet. D'Oyly Carte had built the Savoy Theater especially for Gilbert and Sullivan operettas. After *The Gondoliers* had become a success, Gilbert and Sullivan went on vacation. While they were away, D'Oyly Carte replaced the carpet in the theater and charged all three with the expense.

When Gilbert came home and found out about the cost, he was furious. Sullivan sided with D'Oyly Carte, and Gilbert became furious with both men. The argument was so bitter that it looked as though the partnership would end forever.

It didn't. The two men came together again to create two new operettas: *Utopia Limited* and *The Grand Duke.* They were somewhat successful in their time, but are rarely played nowadays.

Sullivan had been in ill health for years. He wrote some of the later operettas while in great pain. At last, though, his body could take no more. In October 1900, Sullivan died. He was only 58.

Gilbert was a powerful man. He lived on after the death of his younger partner. He continued to play the part of a strong-minded individual, but there was another side to him, a kindly side. Many of his kindnesses were done in private. His short, impatient, often *gruff* tone concealed an inner warmth.

W. S. Gilbert was a man of high principles, honesty, and courage. He showed that side of his character in his last action. On May 29, 1911, two young women came to a lake with Gilbert. He had planned to teach one of the women to swim. Meanwhile, the other woman wandered out too far and yelled, "I am drowning."

Without hesitation Gilbert swam to her side and said, "Put your hands on my shoulders and don't struggle." These were his last words. He disappeared from beneath her grasp. A gardener came with a boat and saved the young woman, but Gilbert was dead. He was 77.

Until a few years ago the D'Oyly Carte Opera Company of London gave regular performances of the operettas. The group has been broken up, but the operettas go on and on across the United States and Great Britain and around the world.

UNDERSTANDING WHAT YOU HAVE READ

Finding Another Title

1. Another good title for this selection might be (a) A History of Operettas (b) Two Geniuses of Comic Opera (c) How Gilbert Met Sullivan (d) The Importance of Good Partnership.

Getting the Main Idea

2. Gilbert and Sullivan (a) enjoyed each other's company (b) could have done without Richard D'Oyly Carte (c) wrote operettas of lasting popularity (d) had similar personalities.

Finding Details

3. Frederic found himself a pirate because of (a) a nursemaid's error (b) his cruel nature (c) his father's friendship with the Pirate King (d) his childhood ambition.
4. A recent movie of *The Pirates of Penzance* featured (a) Madonna (b) Tina Turner (c) Bruce Springsteen (d) Linda Ronstadt.
5. The Lord High Executioner is a character in (a) *The Pirates of Penzance* (b) *H.M.S. Pinafore* (c) *The Mikado* (d) *The Gondoliers*.

6. As a child of two, W. S. Gilbert was kidnapped in (a) England (b) Italy (c) France (d) Spain.
7. The comic opera *Thespis* appeared in (a) 1869 (b) 1871 (c) 1875 (d) 1879.
8. The second operetta produced by Gilbert and Sullivan was (a) *Patience* (b) *The Bab Ballads* (c) *The Sorcerer* (d) *Trial by Jury.*
9. The most important argument between the partners was over a (a) talented young singer (b) sudden change in the plot of an operetta (c) carpet (d) new stage manager.
10. *Utopia Limited* and *The Grand Duke* (a) are popular successes today (b) were written by Gilbert but with somebody else's music (c) are seldom played now (d) are early examples of Gilbert and Sullivan's work.

Making Inferences

11. *The Pirates of Penzance* was probably made into a movie because the producers (a) believed that there were enough Gilbert and Sullivan fans to make the movie popular (b) wanted to pay one last compliment to the memory of Sullivan, not Gilbert (c) tried an experiment with little hope of success (d) were related to W. S. Gilbert.
12. A phrase that might be used to describe the plots of *The Pirates of Penzance* and *The Mikado* is (a) serious complications (b) true-to-life situations (c) boring characters (d) charming nonsense.
13. Gilbert and Sullivan were a success (a) because they had been childhood friends (b) because D'Oyly Carte planned each of their operettas (c) even though Gilbert was lazy and had to be forced

to write   **(d)**   in   spite   of   their   different personalities.

14.   Gilbert probably got the idea for *Trial by Jury* from **(a)** Sullivan   **(b)** his own experiences as a lawyer **(c)** an editor of the magazine *Fun*   **(d)** an experience his father had had.

15.   Sullivan probably never realized that   **(a)** *Ivanhoe* was not as good as *The Mikado*   **(b)** Gilbert tended to be a bossy person   **(c)** Rachel Russell's mother disapproved of him   **(d)** D'Oyly Carte had charged him for part of the carpet.

Predicting What Happens Next

16.   During the periods when a new Gilbert and Sullivan operetta was not yet ready, D'Oyly Carte probably   **(a)** closed the theater   **(b)** broke off his friendship with Gilbert and Sullivan   **(c)** reran former successes   **(d)** told Sullivan that he would write an operetta for him.

Deciding on the Order of Events

17.   The following events are scrambled. Arrange them in proper order, as they happened. Use letters only.
(a) *Thespis* appears at the Gaiety Theater.
(b) Gilbert becomes a lawyer.
(c) *The Sorcerer* is a success.
(d) Sullivan writes "The Lost Chord."

Inferring Tone

18.   When Gilbert spoke to Nellie Farren (73), he was being   **(a)** charming   **(b)** agreeable   **(c)** scornful **(d)** encouraging.

Separating Facts from Opinions

For each of the following, tell whether the statement is a fact (*F*) or an opinion (*O*).

19. Of the two partners, Gilbert had greater skill.
20. Richard D'Oyly Carte put on most of the Gilbert and Sullivan operettas at his Savoy Theater.

Understanding Words from Context

21. They must consider their own success less important than the success of the partnership, or *collaboration,* as it is sometimes called.
   Collaboration (70) calls for   (a) working together   (b) a strong-minded manner   (c) occasional disagreement   (d) good advertising.
22. It was a great success. Sullivan and Burnand were *induced* to put on another operetta.
   Induced (72) means   (a) scared   (b) persuaded   (c) forced   (d) unwilling.
23. Sullivan did not take to Gilbert at all. He avoided him and *declined* a suggestion that he might work with Gilbert on an operetta.
   Declined (73) means   (a) considered carefully   (b) turned down   (c) gladly accepted   (d) wondered at.
24. Though Sullivan was not too eager, he *reluctantly* agreed again and again to work with his difficult partner.
   Reluctantly (75) means   (a) gladly   (b) once upon a time   (c) angrily   (d) unwillingly.
25. During the work on an operetta, there were often disagreements. Sullivan *resented* Gilbert's manner. Gilbert was bothered by Sullivan's hurt feelings.
   Resented (75) means   (a) was amused by   (b) imitated   (c) approved of   (d) was annoyed at.

THINKING IT OVER

1. How did W. S. Gilbert use the experiences in his life to write operettas?
2. Why was the first meeting of Gilbert and Sullivan a failure?
3. "If at first you don't succeed, try, try again." How does this proverb apply to Gilbert?
4. Why is a partnership usually so difficult to manage?
5. Why did Gilbert and Sullivan's partnership succeed?
6. Have you ever seen a Gilbert and Sullivan operetta in the movies or on television? Tell about it.
7. Gilbert was a stern director of his operettas. What is the job of a director? Do you know the names of one or more Hollywood directors? Can you think of a movie directed by the person you mentioned?
8. How did Gilbert show a good side of his character?

ANOTHER LOOK AT THE QUOTATION

> *If you approach each new person you meet in a spirit of adventure, you will find yourself endlessly fascinated by the new channels of thought and experience and personality that you encounter.*
>
> ELEANOR ROOSEVELT

1. Explain the quotation in your own words.
2. Do you agree with the quotation? Have you ever before thought of meeting a new person as an adventure? Explain.

3. Do you think Sullivan would have agreed with Eleanor Roosevelt's advice? How is his agreeing to work with Gilbert in keeping with the spirit of this advice?

WORDS AT YOUR SERVICE—SEQUENCE CLUES

His short, impatient, often gruff *tone concealed an inner warmth. (76)*

Sometimes a sentence gives us a pair or a series of words that provide clues to the meaning of an unfamiliar word. *Short, impatient,* and *gruff* are arranged in a sequence, or series. The arrangement suggests an increasing degree of harshness, from *short* through *impatient* to *gruff.* The word *often* suggests that Gilbert wasn't always gruff. He was more likely to be short or impatient. Sometimes, however, he went a little further. We can guess that the word *gruff* means *rough* and *harsh.*

Sometimes words are paired, with the second one a little stronger than the first:

The babysitter was not only *thoughtless.* She was actually *negligent* in taking care of the child at the playground.

The pairing of *thoughtless* and *negligent* in the context of these two sentences suggests that *negligent* is stronger than *thoughtless. Negligent* suggests a lack of reasonable care.

Study the following sentences and then guess at the meaning of each *italicized* word. Use sequence clues to help you.

EXAMPLE

The day started warm and humid. Within two hours
it was hot. By early afternoon it was *sweltering*.
   Sweltering means   (a) cooling   (b) mild   (c) very
hot   (d) quite pleasant.
   The day is getting hotter and hotter. *Sweltering* must
mean   (c) *very hot*.

1. At first there was a mild uproar in the stadium.
   Then there was *pandemonium*.
   Pandemonium means   (a) confusion and noise   (b)
   joy   (c) sadness   (d) quiet.

2. The Murphys' new house isn't just large. It's *immense*.
   Immense means   (a) ugly   (b) neat and trim   (c)
   huge   (d) bright and cheerful.

3. At first, Norris seemed a little confused by the directions for putting the table together. As he went
   on, he became completely *bewildered*.
   Bewildered means   (a) interested   (b) happy   (c)
   skilled   (d) puzzled.

4. From the beginning, the speaker's story was unlikely, but as he went on, it seemed even more
   farfetched.
   Farfetched means   (a) true-to-life   (b) probably
   untrue   (c) complete   (d) traveling afar.

5. As the lawyer began questioning, there was a crack
   in the witness's calm. After a dozen more questions,
   that calm had completely *disintegrated*.
   Disintegrated means   (a) gone to pieces   (b) returned   (c) given the wrong impression   (d)
   amused the spectators.

MARTINA NAVRATILOVA:

Tennis Superstar

The dictionary is the only place where success comes before work.

ARTHUR BRISBANE

It was early July 1985. The eyes of the tennis world were on Wimbledon, England, and the famous tournament that bears its name. The tournament had been carefully set up. The leading players had been *seeded*. This means that the names of the outstanding players had been spread around so that they would not meet each other early in the tournament. In an ideal tennis tournament, the two best players meet in the final round.

It soon became clear that the men's singles matches were not running true to form. Top seeded players like John McEnroe, Jimmy Connors, and Ivan Lendl were defeated. Lower-ranked players kept winning and moving along. When the dust had cleared, an unseeded 17-year-old player from Germany, Boris Becker, had won the men's singles.

The top seeded players in the women's singles were more fortunate. The two number-one seeds, Martina Navratilova and Chris Evert Lloyd, kept winning. Chris was winning every match easily. Martina, however, had some worries along the way. She had a hard match against Pam Shriver.

Another unseeded player in the women's draw, Molly Van Nostrand of the United States, was moving along. She amazed the tennis world by her sharp play. She defeated the number-four seed, Manuela Maleeva, to enter the quarter finals against Zina Garrison. Her dream ended there, however. She won the first set but lost the next two. Zina moved to the next round.

Zina, an outstanding black athlete from the United States, played Martina in the semifinals. Martina won, but she had to struggle. She had struggled hard in two matches to make the finals. Could she find enough strength to defeat Chris? Just a month earlier she had lost to Chris in the French Open. Chris had also defeated Martina in the Australian Open in December 1984.

Martina said, "I was more of an underdog this time. Chris was a favorite. I had a lot at stake, and if I was going to win, I would have to play my best."

When the match began, Martina was nervous, far from *serene*. On the other side of the court, Chris Evert Lloyd was calm and firm. These two opponents had met many times in the past. They were never more serious in their desire to win than they were now.

The two players have different styles. Chris likes to stay at the baselines, passing her opponents by her accurate shots. Martina likes to rush the net, cutting off her opponents' drives to gain points. At first it looked as though Chris's plan would work best.

Martina rushed the net often, but Chris managed to find openings to pass Martina. Time after time, spectators thought that Martina had made the point. Time after time, Chris got to the ball and angled it for a winning point. Martina had trouble getting her first serve in. The opening set ended with Chris winning 6–4.

Martina seemed to get new life in the second set. Her serves became more accurate. Her game at the net became more effective. She pressed Chris harder and harder. Chris began to make errors, and the tide turned. The game that seemed to make the difference was the ninth. Martina was leading in the set, 5–3, but Chris was ahead in the game, 40–15. Chris needed to win one of the next two points to be back in the match. Martina pressed at the net, and Chris lost the game and the set. Martina then won the next set, 6–2.

After the match was over, Chris was disappointed. She said, "I had chances, but Martina rose to the occasion. This match was disappointing to me because I had beaten her in the French and had played so well here. I felt it was 50–50 going into the match. . . . But I'm not going to pout about it."

Martina said, "This was my most satisfying win. I've lost three matches this year and everyone said I was going downhill. Every year, there is more pressure. Every year, there is so much to prove."

Why did Martina feel so much pressure to win? The better an athlete is, the more people expect of the player. Martina's record through the years has been remarkable. After July 1982 she was rated the number-one tennis player in the world for 156 straight weeks. Chris Evert Lloyd's two important victories before Wimbledon earned her equal ranking with Martina for a while. But the Wimbledon victory put Martina on top again.

Martina's major victories would be too long to list here. Her 1985 victory at Wimbledon was her sixth there, her fourth in a row. In 1984, she received $1 million for winning the four tournaments in a row. These tournaments are the Australian Open, the French Open, Wimbledon, and the U.S. Open.

Martina also has a long list of victories in women's doubles and in mixed doubles. All in all, her record is one of the most incredible in history. But she didn't make a *headlong* trip to become number one. She traveled a long, hard road. This is her story.

Martina Navratilova was born on October 10, 1956, in Prague, Czechoslovakia. She came from a tennis family. Her grandmother was ranked number two in Czechoslovakia. Her stepfather and her mother were tennis officials for the government. Her younger sister is a fine player too.

When Martina was five, the family moved to a suburb of Prague. Her parents played in amateur tennis tournaments every summer. She says, "They were at the courts every day, and they took me with them. I had an old racket that my father cut down, and I hit the ball against a wall. I could do it for hours. They would make me stop and sit me on a chair, but whenever they didn't watch me, I would go to the wall again."

Her stepfather saw that Martina had talent and began to coach her. When she was only eight, she entered a 12-and-under tennis tournament and got as far as the semifinals. By age 14 she had won her first national title. Within the next two years she won three national women's championships. When she won the national junior title, she became the country's leading female tennis player.

While Martina was growing up, her country went through a time of troubles. When Martina was 11 years old, the Russian army invaded Czechoslovakia. Martina was visiting a friend in Pilsen when the Russian tanks came pouring in. She and her friend were terrified. They *cowered* indoors and heard the shooting outside. After dark, her father came on a motorcycle and brought her back to her home outside Prague.

This episode made a deep impression on Martina and may have influenced her later decisions.

In 1973 the United States Lawn Tennis Association invited teams to take part in an eight-week winter tour. The Czechoslovakian Tennis Federation allowed Martina to play. She enjoyed her first visit to the United States. She especially loved pancakes, pizza, and Big Macs. She gained 20 pounds in two months!

When she returned to Europe, she performed well in the Italian Open, Wimbledon, and the French Open. A year later she reached the finals of both the Italian and German Opens. Then it was back to the United States for a tour. She had some important victories..

When Martina returned to Prague again, she was not happy. She was probably the strongest woman in tennis, but she made too many errors. She was impatient, too easy to excite, too easy to upset. She decided to change.

She worked hard to improve her backhand. She slimmed down.

Martina began to defeat players who had beaten her before. She had an unexpected victory over the great Margaret Court in the Australian Open. A month later she defeated Chris Evert Lloyd, who had previously *dominated* her. A few weeks later she defeated Chris again.

By the end of 1975 she had played in the singles finals of seven major tournaments. She had also led the Czech team to victory over the favored Australian team in a Federation Cup match. It was the first Czech team victory in the series since the competition began in 1963.

Martina won almost $200,000 that year, a total second only to Chris's winnings. *Tennis* magazine named her the Most Improved Player of the Year.

For some time Martina had been battling with the Czechoslovakian Tennis Federation. In the United States, the United States Tennis Association is independent. In Czechoslovakia, the Tennis Federation is controlled by the government. The Federation said that Martina was becoming "too Americanized." The officials cut down the number of times she could play in the United States. One way that athletes earn money to keep playing is by saying they like certain products. But officials cut down on her opportunities to *endorse* products for commercials. They refused to allow her to sign up for World Team Tennis, a new sports group in the United States.

Martina explained later, "They told me they didn't want me to play in the United States as much. They actually wanted me to quit tennis for three months and finish school. I was under tension all the time. It didn't matter to them whether I was number one or number 20. They wanted tennis to be second in my life."

Martina came to a difficult decision. She would leave

Czechoslovakia and *defect* to the United States. On September 6, 1975, after losing in the U.S. Open, she asked for asylum—that is, she asked to be allowed to stay in the United States. She said she had no interest in politics, but tennis was her life.

The next year was the most difficult of her life. She was cut off from her home and family. She was lonely and felt *isolated* in a country not her own. She cried often and worried nearly all the time. She said later, "I was lonely. I couldn't turn to my parents for help, but I did have some good friends who helped. I defected because the Czech Tennis Federation wouldn't let me travel, especially to the United States. I was determined to be number one, and if I couldn't come here where 95 percent of the big tournaments are played, I had no chance. Yes, I had talked about it a little with my parents, but I don't think they really believed I would do it. It was my decision, and it was all a question of tennis. There was nothing political about it."

What about her parents? What did they think? Martina said, "My parents had told me if I ever felt I had to leave, not to discuss it. Just go—but make up my mind I'd never be coming back, maybe never see them or my sister Jana again."

The Czech tennis officials didn't forgive her. Newspapers no longer mentioned her name. Other Czech players thought that she had made a bad mistake. Czech officials tried to persuade Martina to change her mind. She felt she couldn't. She thought that if she returned to Czechoslovakia, she would probably never be able to play tennis in the United States again.

In the years that followed, Martina had her ups and downs. If things went wrong, she worried that leaving Czechoslovakia might have been a mistake. Gradually, however, her life changed for the better. She had good friends, like Chris Evert Lloyd and Billie Jean King. Chris was often an opponent and sometimes a doubles partner. Off the courts, Chris was a true friend. She and Billie Jean King helped Martina through many difficult moments.

Martina paid more attention to her physical condition. She stopped eating all that junk food she loved. She changed her diet. She brought her weight down. She whipped herself into excellent physical condition.

As a child, Martina dreamed of being number one in the world in women's tennis. She made that dream come true.

UNDERSTANDING WHAT YOU HAVE READ

Finding Another Title

1. Another good title for this selection might be **(a)** The Wimbledon Tennis Championships **(b)** Chris and Martina—Two Friendly Opponents **(c)** How Winning Tennis Is Played **(d)** The Rise of a Great Tennis Champion.

Getting the Main Idea

2. Martina **(a)** did not have an easy time reaching the top in tennis **(b)** probably would have won at Wimbledon even if she had stayed in Czechoslovakia **(c)** is basically a calm, unemotional person **(d)** should not have left her home to move to the United States.

Finding Details

3. All these players were defeated at Wimbledon in 1985 EXCEPT **(a)** John McEnroe **(b)** Boris Becker **(c)** Jimmy Connors **(d)** Ivan Lendl.
4. Molly Van Nostrand **(a)** was a highly seeded player **(b)** defeated Manuela Maleeva **(c)** played against Martina **(d)** easily defeated Zina Garrison.
5. The game that seemed to make the difference in the second set between Chris and Martina was **(a)** the fifth **(b)** the seventh **(c)** the ninth **(d)** the eleventh.
6. Martina's number-one world ranking began in **(a)** 1978 **(b)** 1980 **(c)** 1982 **(d)** 1984.
7. All the following are mentioned as "Grand Slam" tournaments EXCEPT **(a)** the Italian Open **(b)** the French Open **(c)** Wimbledon **(d)** the Australian Open.
8. Martina won her first national title at the age of **(a)** five **(b)** eight **(c)** 12 **(d)** 14.
9. Martina defeated Margaret Court **(a)** at Wimbledon **(b)** in the Australian Open **(c)** in the German Open **(d)** in the U.S. Open.
10. The Czech team won a victory over Australia in **(a)** 1963 **(b)** 1973 **(c)** 1975 **(d)** 1977.

Making Inferences

11. At the beginning of the Wimbledon tournaments no one expected that **(a)** Molly Van Nostrand would reach the quarter finals **(b)** Martina and Chris would meet in the finals **(c)** John McEnroe would reach the finals **(d)** Ivan Lendl would win.

12. Many experts thought that Chris would win the Wimbledon finals because **(a)** she had beaten Martina in the last four Wimbledon finals **(b)** Martina had gained too much weight **(c)** Martina had changed the way she played **(d)** Martina had struggled through several matches to reach the finals.

13. Martina owes a great debt to her **(a)** sister Jana **(b)** stepfather **(c)** grandmother **(d)** friend in Pilsen.

14. When Martina left Czechoslovakia for the United States, what she wanted most was **(a)** a new car **(b)** good publicity in Czech newspapers **(c)** freedom to play tennis **(d)** a free supply of new tennis rackets.

15. Chris's treatment of Martina during Martina's difficult time was **(a)** admirable **(b)** unfriendly **(c)** strange **(d)** humorous.

Predicting What Happens Next

16. After losing in the semifinals at Wimbledon, Zina Garrison probably **(a)** gave up tennis **(b)** stayed away from tennis for six months to recover **(c)** invited Molly Van Nostrand to tour Europe with her **(d)** planned to play again at Wimbledon.

Deciding on the Order of Events

17. The following events are scrambled. Arrange them in proper order, as they happened. Use letters only.
    (a) Molly Van Nostrand defeats Manuela Maleeva.
    (b) Martina defeats Chris in 1985 in the Wimbledon finals.
    (c) Martina asks to stay in the United States.
    (d) Russian tanks move into Czechoslovakia.

Inferring Tone

18. When Martina talked about the year after she left Czechoslovakia (90), her tone was (a) lively (b) comical (c) sad (d) bored.

Separating Facts from Opinions

For each of the following, tell whether the statement is a fact (*F*) or an opinion (*O*).

19. The French Open is one of the "Grand Slam" tournaments.
20. The French Open is more important than the Australian Open.

Understanding Words from Context

21. She and her friend were terrified. They *cowered* indoors and heard the shooting outside.
    Cowered (88) means (a) shouted (b) played games (c) moved around (d) crouched in fear.
22. A month later she defeated Chris Evert Lloyd, who had previously *dominated* her.
    Dominated (89) means (a) controlled (b) spoken to (c) spoken about (d) answered.
23. One way that athletes earn money to keep playing is by saying they like certain products. But officials cut down on her opportunities to *endorse* products for commercials.
    Endorse (89) means (a) taste (b) approve (c) criticize (d) enjoy.
24. She would leave Czechoslovakia and *defect* to the United States.
    Defect (90) means (a) give up one's country for another (b) find a way to improve relationships

(c) try another solution to a problem (d) win approval for a good idea.

25. She was lonely and felt *isolated* in a country not her own.

    Isolated (90) means (a) cheerful but a little worried (b) famous but misunderstood (c) alone and set apart (d) weak and trembling.

THINKING IT OVER

1. How did Martina rise above troubles to become a success in tennis?

2. At the beginning of her career, Martina often gave up if she fell behind. How did she prove she had overcome that weakness in the Wimbledon final?

3. What are some of the good things about being number one in the world? What are some of the disadvantages? Would you like to be number one in some sport? Why or why not?

4. Some experts say that the difference between a good athlete and a great athlete has to do with mental qualities. Great athletes can give their full attention to what they are doing. They have confidence in their abilities. Who, in your opinion, is a great athlete in a sport other than tennis? Does this person show superior mental abilities?

5. Baseball, football, and basketball are team sports. How does tennis differ? Is an individual sport or a team sport more tense? How else are these two areas of sports different?

6. What is your favorite sport to watch on television? Why?

7. When players travel across the seas, they experience jet lag. Can you explain what jet lag is? Why is it a problem?
8. At Wimbledon, there are matches in men's singles, women's singles, men's doubles, women's doubles, and mixed doubles. Yet the singles matches always get the most publicity and the most spectators. Why?

ANOTHER LOOK AT THE QUOTATION

> *The dictionary is the only place where success comes before work.*
> ARTHUR BRISBANE

1. Explain the quotation in your own words.
2. Did Martina earn her success through hard work? Explain.
3. Have you had an experience in which hard work brought success to you in some activity? Tell about it.

WORDS AT YOUR SERVICE—ANTONYMS AND CONTRAST

> *When the match began, Martina was nervous, far from* serene. *(86)*

Even if *serene* is a new word for you, the sentence tells you it is an antonym, or opposite, of *nervous*. Contrast shows differences. The word *nervous* contrasts the way Martina really felt with the way she could have felt, *serene*.

Sometimes the contrast is not created by an antonym, but by a phrase or a sentence, as in the following:

> *She didn't make a* headlong *trip to become number one. She traveled a long, hard road. (87)*

The second sentence tells you that *headlong* is the opposite of *long, hard. Headlong* must mean something like *swift, rapid, without delay.*

Study the following sentences and then guess at the meaning of each *italicized* word. Use the antonym or contrast in the sentence to help you.

EXAMPLE

a. The schemes of the people selling land were *fraudulent,* not honest.
   Fraudulent means **(a)** respectable **(b)** crooked **(c)** interesting **(d)** profitable.
   Not tells us that *honest* is an antonym of *fraudulent.* Therefore, the correct answer is **(b)** *crooked.*

b. Every child would rather be *coddled* than treated harshly.
   Coddled means **(a)** scolded **(b)** punished **(c)** treated tenderly **(d)** annoyed.
   Coddled is contrasted with harsh treatment. Therefore, the answer is **(c)** *treated tenderly.*

1. Doreen's reasons for leaving her job were not clear to her parents, but they were *obvious* to me.
   Obvious means **(a)** poor **(b)** silly **(c)** puzzling **(d)** plain.

2. His writing was a model of *clarity,* but his speech was confused.
   Clarity means **(a)** clearness **(b)** speed **(c)** humor **(d)** mix-up.

3. It is *customary,* not unusual, for a judge to wear a wig in a British courtroom.
   Customary means **(a)** usual **(b)** comforting **(c)** unpleasant **(d)** proud.
4. After enjoying a *strenuous* half-hour of exercise, I like a relaxing period at the side of the pool.
   Strenuous means **(a)** quiet **(b)** humorous **(c)** wasted **(d)** active.
5. Nicholas's employer had a *volcanic* temper, not a gentle manner at all.
   Volcanic means **(a)** lovable **(b)** explosive **(c)** controlled **(d)** easygoing.

KAREEM ABDUL-JABBAR:
Basketball Star

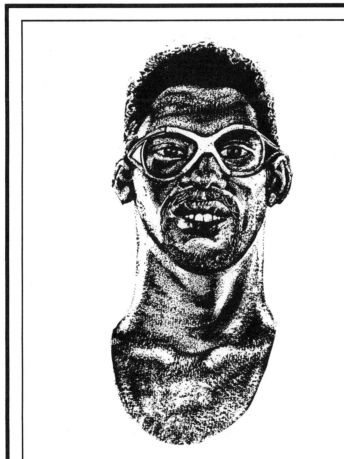

Sports do not build character. They reveal it.

HEYWOOD HALE BROUN

99

It was 1985. The Los Angeles Lakers were coming to the Boston Garden to play the sixth game of the basketball finals. The Lakers were ahead, three games to two, but they did not feel sure of the outcome. Eight times in the past the Lakers and the Boston Celtics had met in the championship finals of the National Basketball Association. Never, since 1959, had the Lakers defeated the Celtics in the championship series. Eight times they had lost the championship. Just a year earlier they had lost in seven games to the Celtics.

Basketball writers were saying the Lakers were jinxed when they played against the Celtics. Somehow the Lakers played excellent basketball in other playoff games. But when they met the Celtics, they seemed to find ways to lose.

This is how the important series developed. The first two games of the 1985 series were played in Boston. The Celtics buried the Lakers in Game 1. The Lakers bounded back. They won the second game in Boston and the third game in Los Angeles. At this point they had a 2–1 lead in the series, but the Celtics came back to tie the series at 2 all. Game 4 was a heartbreaker for the Lakers. The score was 107–105. With only two seconds left to play, the Celtics made the winning goal.

With the game score tied at 2–2, the Lakers had to play one more game in Los Angeles. If they lost, they'd return to Boston behind 3–2.

In Game 5 the Lakers began to take control. At halftime they were ahead 64–51, but the Celtics never gave up. With a little more than six minutes left, they came within four points—at 101–97. The Lakers hung on and won 120–111. The game score at this point favored the Lakers 3–2.

The Lakers had to fly back to Boston for the final game or games. They could end the series by beating the Celtics in Game 6. But they could lose the series if the Celtics won in Games 6 and 7. The Boston Garden had been a *graveyard* for them before. Could they recover to win now?

Some sportswriters felt that the Lakers were full of energy, while the Celtics were tired. In the first game of the series, the Celtics had shot a record 60.8 percent of their baskets from the floor. In the sixth game, they shot only 38.5 percent.

Game 6 began. For the first half of Game 6, the score was very close. At halftime the teams were tied at 55. Then some of the players on both teams began to tire. One person, however, stood out. Kareem Abdul-Jabbar, at 38, was "an old man" by many athletic standards. But it was Kareem who, in the sixth game, led his Lakers to victory—and to the championship. He scored 18 of his 29 points in the second half and actually seemed to get stronger as the game went on.

Kareem isn't impressed with his success as an older player. He said, "The best marathoner in the world is in his thirties. He pays the price. I live with me all the time. I know what I can do." The marathon, a long-distance run, demands the ability to last through the long race. It takes a great deal of strength and *stamina*. So does professional basketball.

The Lakers won, 111–100. They broke the old jinx. They proved that a team could beat the champion Celtics on their own home ground. Most of all, Kareem Abdul-Jabbar showed that he could still play basketball better than the best of them. He was the *unanimous* choice as the playoffs' Most Valuable Player. No one voted against him.

At 38, Kareem could look back on a long life of basketball. He was born Lew Alcindor on April 16, 1947. In 1971, he changed his name to Kareem Abdul-Jabbar, but in his early career he was known simply as Lew.

Kareem spent his childhood in New York City. He was a sports fan, especially of the Brooklyn Dodgers baseball team. In 1955, when Kareem was in the third grade, the Brooklyn Dodgers beat the New York Yankees in the World Series. Since most of his friends were Yankee fans, Kareem had a happy winter glorying in his team's victory. He was also a fan of the New York football Giants. When he was in the seventh and eighth grades, he went to all their games. His number as a Laker, 33, was the number of Mel Triplett, his favorite Giant player.

He also played baseball in Little League. He pitched and played centerfield for his team and won a trophy for his *participation*. It was basketball, though, that shaped his life.

Kareem grew rapidly and soon was taller than his classmates. "You should play basketball," people told him, and he did. He later recalled, "I was about eight, and I was in the fourth grade at grammar school and was about five feet tall, when they began telling me [to play basketball]. It really began paying off more when I was thirteen. I was six-seven then."

At this time he won a scholarship to Power Memorial Academy, and his life was never the same. A scholarship is a grant of money for study. At 15 he was seven feet tall. Wherever he went, people noticed him. He said a little sadly, "I never could be me. I lost my privacy."

Naturally, while Kareem was still in high school, college and professional scouts kept an eye on him. Kareem went to Wilt Chamberlain, then a star with Philadelphia, for advice. As Wilt said later, "I never tried to persuade him about a college or anything else. I just told him what it had been like for me and let him take it from there." Later these two players would struggle against each other on the courts. Wilt was then an experienced player. Kareem was a new basketball star.

For his college, Kareem chose UCLA, the University of California at Los Angeles. He played for famous coach John Wooden. He starred on the UCLA team. In 1968 he came to New York to play in the Holiday Festival at Madison Square Garden. Since he had played in the Far West, few New York fans had had a chance to see him. Madison Square Garden was filled with scouts, former players, and fans who hoped Kareem would some day join the Knicks. Kareem played well and showed what he might do as a professional.

Still, many people doubted his ability. There is a great difference between college and pro basketball. In pro basketball every player has been selected from the thousands of college players. The pro game is rough. Players must be able to take a lot of physical abuse. The struggle under the basket for a rebound, a ball that bounces off the rim, is a physical battle. Some players cannot take it. Could Kareem, who was a slender giant, survive?

Kareem graduated and became *eligible* to be chosen for the 1969 selection of players. The Milwaukee Bucks won the rights to Kareem. He was signed for a figure estimated at $1.5 million.

Kareem played six seasons for Milwaukee. Five times his team was in the playoffs. As time went on, though, Kareem tired of the Bucks. He asked to be traded.

Since Kareem was a New York athlete, the New York Knicks tried hard to get him, but there were misunderstandings.

The New York Knickerbockers hoped to get their hometown boy on their team. But somehow they were never able to make the deal. As a professional, Kareem often played against the New York Knicks. Red Holzman, the famous coach of that team, said, "Kareem always seemed to be a very private person to me. In all the years he has been in the league, few words have been exchanged between us. But he had my respect. He had a certain quiet dignity that I liked. Not once in all the years of losing important games to the Knicks and listening to his hometown New York fans boo him, did I know him to complain. Not once did I hear him alibi."

Although Kareem became famous early in life, he always kept his calm, quiet dignity. Nearly everyone who has known Kareem has only good things to say about him. His high school coach said, "There are none better to coach, not only as a player but as a person. I have a rule on my team. A player who scores a basket has to thank the man who threw him the pass." This rule made an impression on Kareem.

Kareem went to the Los Angeles Lakers instead of the Knicks. They gave $1 million to Milwaukee, plus four players, for Kareem and another player.

In his very first season with Los Angeles, he helped bring the team to the playoffs. There were many playoffs after that, as Kareem and his team swept through their opponents. But every time the Lakers came up against the Celtics, they lost. There were heartbreaking finishes and losses by narrow margins. But the Celtics, time after time, defeated the Lakers in the finals. That is, until 1985.

Soon after the 1985 playoffs, Bryant Gumbel interviewed Kareem on the NBC *Today* show. Bryant introduced Kareem as the highest scorer in NBA regular season play as well as in the playoffs. He mentioned Kareem's six record-breaking Most Valuable Player awards. Then he said, "You are 38. In the rest of the world you are a very young man, and yet in basketball everyone kept on talking about how old Kareem Abdul-Jabbar was. Does that bother you?"

"No," Kareem replied. "It doesn't bother me. I understand it because no one has played regularly at my age in the NBA. No one. . . . So here I am starting every game and playing at the top of my profession."

"How do you explain it?"

Kareem smiled and said, "I pay a price. I work very hard in the summer to keep in condition."

The interview also brought out the special warmth of Kareem as he spoke about his young son. The question of Kareem's height (over seven feet) came up, too.

As Kareem pointed out, many tall players never reached the top. In a book called *On Court with the Superstars of the NBA,* Kareem talked about his height and his job as center.

"My height is an advantage to me on the court, but not so much as most fans seem to think. I believe that a center has more responsibility on a basketball team than any other player, to start with. You're the biggest, so you're supposed to score the most points. You're also supposed to do the most rebounding, the most screening for your teammates, and another job you have is to keep plays moving with your passing."

Kareem has tried to expand his skills. In the early 1980s Kareem had a small role in the movie *Airplane.* In it he played a co-pilot. Peter Graves played a pilot. The movie was one of the funniest of the year. Kareem showed his great sense of humor and comic-acting skill.

What type of athlete is Kareem Abdul-Jabbar? When Kareem was a young player of 22, he had to play against Willis Reed. Reed was a strong *veteran,* with many years' experience in pro basketball. One night he paid Kareem the perfect tribute. He said, "Good thing I don't have to play him every night. One day, the guy is going to wake up and find out how really good he is. I just hope he doesn't. He's got all that equipment. It's great to have that much height and all those skills."

Sixteen years later, Kareem knew how good he was.

UNDERSTANDING WHAT YOU HAVE READ

Finding Another Title

1. Another good title for this selection might be **(a)** How Basketball Is Played in the NBA **(b)** The Lakers–Celtics Finals **(c)** The Lakers' Amazing Basketball Star **(d)** A Long-Time Rivalry.

Getting the Main Idea

2. Kareem Abdul-Jabbar is **(a)** an outstanding athlete **(b)** a lucky player **(c)** a slow starter but a fast finisher **(d)** an angry person.

Finding Details

3. The first two games of the 1985 championship were played in **(a)** Milwaukee **(b)** Boston **(c)** Los Angeles **(d)** New York.
4. The final score of the fifth game was **(a)** 101–97 **(b)** 111–100 **(c)** 55–55 **(d)** 120–111.
5. In the final game of the 1985 series, Kareem scored most of his points in **(a)** the first quarter **(b)** the first half **(c)** the third quarter **(d)** the second half.
6. Kareem changed his name in **(a)** 1947 **(b)** 1955 **(c)** 1971 **(d)** 1975.
7. A boyhood football hero of Kareem's was **(a)** Mel Triplett **(b)** John Wooden **(c)** Bryant Gumbel **(d)** Willis Reed.
8. The person Kareem went to for advice was **(a)** Red Holzman **(b)** Wilt Chamberlain **(c)** John Wooden **(d)** Willis Reed.

9. The total number of seasons Kareem played for Milwaukee was **(a)** four **(b)** five **(c)** six **(d)** seven.

10. All the following descriptions can be applied to Kareem EXCEPT **(a)** the highest scorer in the NBA regular season play **(b)** the highest scorer in a single game in the playoffs **(c)** the oldest active player in the NBA **(d)** winner of six awards for Most Valuable Player.

Making Inferences

11. The Lakers were especially glad to win the 1985 championship series because **(a)** Kareem had a personal enemy on the Celtics team **(b)** they had never beaten the Celtics in a championship series before **(c)** they played the last two games in Los Angeles, their hometown **(d)** their coach didn't think they could win.

12. The comparison between the Celtics' scores in the first and sixth games suggests that they **(a)** gave up trying **(b)** were worn out from the pressure of the series **(c)** counted too much on luck **(d)** tried too many show-off shots.

13. Kareem compared himself to a marathon runner because he and the marathoner **(a)** have been close friends for years **(b)** had the same trainer **(c)** were both in the 1976 Olympics **(d)** are both thought old as athletes.

14. The statement about "the champion Celtics on their own home ground" (101) suggests that **(a)** the Celtics win most of their home games **(b)** the Celtics play poorly at home **(c)** other teams enjoy coming into the Boston Garden **(d)** the Lakers have won more games than the Celtics in Boston.

15. When Willis Reed (105) talks about "all that equipment," he is referring to Kareem's (a) training weights (b) basketball shoes (c) physical abilities (d) outfit with the number 33.

Predicting What Happens Next

16. After the 1985 basketball season, Kareem probably (a) decided to retire (b) asked to be traded to the Celtics (c) started training for the next season (d) turned down the Most Valuable Player award.

Deciding on the Order of Events

17. The following events are scrambled. Arrange them in proper order, as they happened. Use letters only.
    (a) Kareem is given a scholarship to Power Memorial Academy.
    (b) Kareem helps the Lakers defeat the Celtics in the championship game.
    (c) Kareem goes to Milwaukee.
    (d) Kareem goes to UCLA.

Inferring Attitude

18. The attitude of Red Holzman (103) toward Kareem is one of (a) annoyance (b) admiration (c) unfriendliness (d) uncertainty.

Separating Facts from Opinions

For each of the following, tell whether the statement is a fact (F) or an opinion (O).
19. At 15 Kareem was already seven feet tall.
20. Kareem was still playing at 38.

Understanding Words from Context

21. The marathon, a long-distance run, demands the ability to last through the long race. It takes a great deal of strength and *stamina.*
    Stamina (101) means (a) special talent (b) staying power (c) sense of humor (d) cheerful manner.

22. He was the *unanimous* choice as the playoffs' Most Valuable Player. No one voted against him.
    Unanimous (101) means (a) with everyone agreeing (b) last-minute (c) most unexpected (d) most deserving.

23. He pitched and played centerfield for his team and won a trophy for his *participation.*
    Participation (102) means (a) coach (b) manager (c) taking part (d) many home runs.

24. Kareem graduated and became *eligible* to be chosen in the 1969 selection of players.
    Eligible (103) means (a) unwilling (b) angry (c) overlooked (d) qualified.

25. Reed was a strong *veteran,* with many years' experience in pro basketball.
    Veteran (105) means someone (a) playing for the first time (b) chosen by coaches of other teams (c) with long experience (d) with very little success.

THINKING IT OVER

1. What special characteristics did Kareem have as a basketball player?

2. How was he able to play long after most basketball players his age had to retire?

3. Do you believe in jinxes in sports? Can you think of another example of a jinx—perhaps a great hitter who cannot hit against a certain pitcher or a good team that has difficulty beating a weaker team?

4. Some sports figures make salaries in the millions of dollars. Do you believe that some athletes are overpaid? Explain.

5. Now and then, athletes in a major sport decide to strike. Do you think athletes should strike? Explain.

6. Sports seasons are longer than they used to be. In baseball, for example, the World Series used to start at the beginning of October. Nowadays it begins much later. Playoff matches take up more and more time. Do you think some of these seasons are too long? Explain.

7. Which sport do you think requires the most skill? The best physical condition? The most courage? Explain.

8. Football coach Vince Lombardi once said, "Winning isn't everything. It's the *only* thing." What did he mean? Do you agree? Can winning be made to seem too important? Explain.

ANOTHER LOOK AT THE QUOTATION

Sports do not build character. They reveal it.

HEYWOOD HALE BROUN

1. Explain the quotation in your own words.

2. Do you think sports build character? If so, how?

3. Which do you think are better for building character—team sports like baseball, or individual sports like tennis? Explain.

4. Give examples of athletes who show good character and are good role models for young people. Explain why you selected these athletes.

WORDS AT YOUR SERVICE—DENOTATION AND CONNOTATION

> *The Boston Garden had been a* grave-yard *for them before. Could they recover to win this time?* (101)

A *graveyard* is a cemetery. Clearly the Lakers were not going to a cemetery. What does the sentence mean? A graveyard suggests gloom, quiet, loneliness, defeat, and death. The writer of the sentence wanted to suggest the failure of the Lakers in previous playoff games in the Boston Garden.

The use of *graveyard* illustrates two different meanings of the word. The dictionary definition is called *denotation*. The denotation of *graveyard* is simple: *a burial ground.*

There are other meanings that gather around a word. As a word is used, it picks up associations and emotional feelings, extra meanings. We call these extra meanings *connotations*. The denotation of *graveyard* is direct and simple. But the connotation of the word is negative. It arouses unpleasant feelings and associations in most people.

Connotations vary for people. For some, the word *cat* has pleasant connotations—of a beautiful animal, dignified and well mannered. For others the word *cat* has unpleasant connotations—of a dangerous animal with sharp claws and an unfriendly manner. Is the connotation of *cat,* for you, pleasant or unpleasant?

Study each of the following pairs of words. Tell which word in each pair has the more pleasant connotation for you. Explain why.

1. home—house
2. animal—beast
3. hut—shack
4. flower—lily
5. horse—nag

6. cabin—tent
7. cowboy—shepherd
8. garden—lawn
9. friend—pal
10. dog—puppy

Which of the following words have an unpleasant connotation for you? Explain why.

1. football
2. garlic
3. gasoline
4. hound
5. insect

6. Labor Day
7. Monday
8. peas
9. stone
10. worm

DEBBIE ALLEN:
Actress, Dancer, Choreographer

*All that we send into the lives of others
comes back into our own.*

EDWIN MARKHAM

When we watch performers on television, we may secretly envy their work. They seem to have such a relaxed, happy time of it. They speak their lines with easy self-confidence. If they dance or sing, they seem to do so with little effort. The actual facts are quite different, though.

When the idea for the television series *Fame* was born, Debbie Allen won a job at once. Because she had successfully starred in the movie *Fame,* she was hired to act and dance. Soon her other talents were apparent to the producers. She was given additional jobs. She became a choreographer for the company. That is, she was responsible for working out the dance routines. She was also given a job managing the dance company.

Working at all these jobs was a back-breaking task. Debbie said, "If somebody drops out, I have to audition and look for other people. I have to go to production meetings. I have to talk about lights, costumes, sets, and what other people's shoes look like. It's an incredible amount of work."

There's enough work just in acting, let alone in handling the other jobs. Rehearsals would be called at six in the morning. Lines would be learned. Then the script would be changed at the last minute. Debbie said, "You're always perfecting up until the last minute. The real body of the work is beat up and mixed up in a lot of sweat, blood, and tears. Anyone who talks about the glamour of this profession should experience a show like *Fame* to know that the glamour is only icing on the cake."

Why take on the extra jobs? Why didn't Debbie concentrate on acting and dancing? Of course, she appreciated the extra money. But her reasons ran deeper. She believed in the show. She thought it had a good effect. It showed people of many races and religions working together. She gave her opinion in this way: "We're lucky because we're not doing your average television show.

We're doing a show that has a great *impact,* a positive *impact* on people. I mean you see black people, white people, Puerto Rican people that happen to be different, but we're all relating as people."

The series *Fame* had an unusual life. It was immediately recognized as a quality show. Major television critics called it their favorite show. It won 12 Emmy nominations in 1982 and won awards in five different categories. Young people in big cities took to it at once. But it didn't catch on with the public as a whole.

In England *Fame* became the number-one weekly TV show. The English called for stage appearances by Debbie. But in the United States, *Fame* did not draw a 30 percent share of the audience. This number is considered necessary to keep a show on the air. Unfortunately, *Fame* ran against the popular *Magnum, P.I.* Kay Dangaard, public relations officer for *Fame,* admitted, "*Magnum* is one of our really big problems."

Still *Fame* was kept on the air for a while longer. Top management at NBC-TV supported it. The network's program chief, Brandon Tartikoff, firmly believed that there is an audience for good television. Still, without improved ratings, the show couldn't go on forever. It was dropped—and then picked up again for syndication. Old shows were sold on an individual basis to stations around the country. To meet the demand, new shows were filmed. Although *Fame* did not get a prime-time network slot, it appeared on a great many stations throughout the United States.

The show took on new life. Older performers graduated, and new performers like Nia Peeples and Jesse Borrego took over.

Where did this long-lived series spring from? Many TV series are spinoffs from movies or other television series. The long-running *The Jeffersons,* for example, was a spinoff from the very popular *All in the Family*. Some spinoffs last a very short time. Others, like *The Jeffersons,* prove as successful as the originals.

The TV series *Fame* is a spinoff from the movie *Fame*. This movie was released by MGM in 1980. In it Debbie Allen played Lydia Grant, a dance teacher at New York City's High School of Performing Arts. In the TV series her role was enlarged and made more important. As writer Charles Sanders noted, "She [Debbie] is featured weekly as the energetic, hard-driving, no-nonsense teacher who not only shapes a group of teenagers into a precision dance ensemble but who also is often involved in their personal crises and personal joys." *Precision dancing* is perfect dancing, without mistakes. An *ensemble* is a group.

"She's a lot like that in real life, too," says Gene Anthony Ray. He's a young New Yorker who plays Leroy on the show. He explained, "You learn how to really dance when you work with her, and you learn a lot about professionalism. She's all business when it comes to her work; she *does not play*. But when you need her to be your friend, when you need someone to talk out a problem or share a secret, she's always there."

Ray paused a moment and then said, "And she doesn't allow anybody among the dancers to play that 'I'm a star' thing with her. She lets you know right away that she's the choreographer, and she can bring you right back down to earth on the same level with everyone else. What she preaches is the *perfection* of your art and doing what professionalism dictates that you *must* do."

Professionalism is a sense of pride in work. It's an effort to do the best you can at every moment. It's a willingness to make your own interests less important than the interests of the entire group. It's unselfishness, or thinking of others, combined with talent and skill. It's the ability to do your job even when you're tired or out of sorts.

Whoever speaks about Debbie Allen seems to use the word *professionalism*. Erica Gimpel, who is Coco on the show, said, "What I like about her is her professionalism and how she's always so *straightforward* about everything—especially about what she wants as choreographer of the show. She's very tough but very honest at all times."

Remember that she had to deal with young, lively dancers who had minds of their own. They soon learned to respect this gentle-but-tough young woman. Derrick Brice, a dancer on *Fame,* said, "She can be a lot of fun when we're on break or off the set, but when she calls us back to work, all the kidding stops and it's strictly business and professionalism with her."

In the summer of 1985, Debbie appeared in a revival of *Sweet Charity.* This assignment forced her to cut down on her other activities. As she said, "It was the hardest thing putting this [*Sweet Charity*] together and working out my schedule because I'm really involved in *Fame* in so many different ways. . . . I don't choreograph and direct while I'm doing *Sweet Charity*—that's impossible—but I'll act and I'll dance and I'll be Miss Grant between the hours of 9 A.M. and 5 P.M."

Where did Debbie Allen come from? How did she get to be the way she is? What experiences did she have along the way? She gained success the hard way. She earned it.

She was born in January 1953 and grew up in Houston, Texas. Her parents were divorced many years ago. Her father, Dr. Andrew A. Allen, is a Houston dentist. Her mother, Vivian Ayers, is a poet who was nominated for a Pulitzer Prize in 1952. Her sister, Phylicia Rashad, is a gifted actress. She plays Cosby's wife on the highly successful *The Cosby Show.* Her older brother, Tex Allen, is a famous jazz trumpeter and *composer.* Her younger brother, Hugh Weldon Allen, is a student at the University of Texas.

The family is very close. As Phylicia explained, "We grew up understanding that if one of us made it, we all made it. One success was a success for everybody."

Dr. Allen is proud of Debbie's attitude toward success. He said that she's "the same Debbie despite all her success. She hasn't changed a bit, and I'm grateful for that."

Her mother said, "Part of her genius is the tremendous faith she has always had—faith in herself and in the vision of America. She has always believed she could make 'the American Dream' work for her benefit, too, and she has done that. I'm proud of her and what *all* my children have accomplished."

Her belief in the American Dream caused her to try out for all kinds of parts. Most roles, after all, can be played by black or white actors. She said, "In the movies there are many parts that I can play that are not written 'Black.'"

Debbie was greatly influenced by her parents. Her father encouraged her throughout her schooling. Her mother provided many extra advantages. She once took her children to Mexico City for a year so that they could understand how other people live.

During her senior year in high school, Debbie *auditioned* for the North Carolina School of the Arts. The teachers liked her dancing, but they rejected her. She was crushed. She stopped dancing for a whole year and almost gave it up for good. She went to Howard University, in Washington, D.C., and graduated with honors. She had a bachelor's degree in speech and drama.

While Debbie was at Howard, Mike Malone of Washington's Mike Malone Dancers started her dancing again. She danced with student groups. She spent summers attending dance festivals. She met many of the great dancers and choreographers of the time—Alvin Ailey, Martha Graham, Twyla Tharp, Donald McKayle, and Talley Beatty. They all thought she was talented. She got over the hurt she felt when the North Carolina School of the Arts rejected her.

Debbie began her professional career in New York. She was in the chorus line of *Purlie.* She danced with the George Faison troupe. She got enthusiastic reviews for her role as Anita in the 1980 revival of *West Side Story.* She had important parts in many other musicals.

Debbie had important acting roles, too. She got excellent reviews for her stage role in *Raisin in the Sun.* She played Alex Haley's wife in the TV miniseries *Roots II.* She also played in the films *The Fish That Saved Pittsburgh* and *Ragtime,* as well as in the movie *Fame.*

Debbie somehow manages to combine her professional career and her personal life. In 1984, a child, Vivian Nicole, was born to Debbie and her husband, Norm Nixon, basketball star. She confesses that her life was unbelievably busy even before the baby, but she tries to fit everything in. In an interview in *Jet* magazine, she said, "I find time to fix breakfast and dinner, and we sit down at the table as a family. . . . And there are always the weekends."

Debbie is a spokesperson for black performers. She feels her success has helped other black actors and dancers. But there is a long road ahead. She has said, "We need black people in all the positions—on camera, behind the camera, producing, directing . . . everywhere."

She feels that *Fame* makes an important point. "It's a show that's all about people—and their blackness or whiteness or whatever doesn't really enter into the stories most of the time. It's about kids being together and working out their problems, which is the way I wish the world really could be."

Debbie has a dance poster in her Hollywood apartment. It reads, in part, "Dancing is the *loftiest*, the most moving, the most beautiful of the arts. It is no mere translation of life. . . . It is life itself."

To Debbie, dancing *is* life itself.

UNDERSTANDING WHAT YOU HAVE READ

Finding Another Title

1. Another good title for this selection might be **(a)** How *Fame* Was Written **(b)** Artist of the Dance **(c)** The Problems of Television **(d)** An Interesting Story.

Getting the Main Idea

2. Debbie Allen **(a)** once played in *Ragtime* and *Roots* **(b)** would rather act than dance **(c)** feels that her life's work is very worthwhile **(d)** knows how to take it easy on the set.

Finding Details

3. In the television series *Fame*, Debbie Allen had all the following jobs EXCEPT **(a)** set designer **(b)** actress **(c)** dancer **(d)** choreographer.
4. Debbie believes in the show *Fame* because **(a)** it shows people of all races and colors working together **(b)** it successfully challenged *Magnum, P.I.*

in the ratings (c) it was her first acting job (d) her friends said it was a good show.

5. *Fame* was especially successful with (a) children in country areas (b) French listeners (c) older people in city areas (d) young people in big cities.

6. The word people apply most often to Debbie Allen is (a) *humor* (b) *professionalism* (c) *management* (d) *relaxation.*

7. The person who plays Coco on *Fame* is (a) Gene Anthony Ray (b) Derrick Brice (c) Erica Gimpel (d) Kay Dangaard.

8. Phylicia Rashad is Debbie's (a) sister (b) mother (c) best friend (d) aunt.

9. The person who started Debbie dancing again after her disappointment was (a) Brandon Tartikoff (b) Mike Malone (c) George Faison (d) Twyla Tharp.

10. Debbie played Anita in (a) *Purlie* (b) *Raisin in the Sun* (c) *West Side Story* (d) *Fame,* the movie.

Making Inferences

11. The selection suggests that television performers (a) are chosen through favoritism (b) have an easy, pleasant time of it (c) are brighter, on the average, than movie actors (d) work very hard.

12. *Fame* might have had stronger ratings if it (a) had not been up against *Magnum, P.I.* (b) had bigger names in the cast (c) had the full support of management at NBC (d) had better scripts.

13. A television spinoff (a) uses characters from an older series in new situations (b) is almost always more successful than the original (c) is rarely tried on network TV (d) does not use any actors from the original program.

14. Debbie's experience in North Carolina probably caused her to **(a)** decide not to go to college **(b)** lose confidence in herself **(c)** go straight to New York to become an actress **(d)** dance more often for the next year.

15. Debbie feels that her achievements **(a)** are greater than those of her sister or brother **(b)** are not too important, after all **(c)** prove that black people can fit in anywhere in television **(d)** were made possible by Twyla Tharp.

Predicting What Happens Next

16. As the work in *Fame* began to wind down, Debbie Allen probably **(a)** applied a second time to the school that had once rejected her **(b)** moved to England to live there permanently **(c)** joined the cast of *The Cosby Show* **(d)** had many other job offers.

Deciding on the Order of Events

17. The following events are scrambled. Arrange them in proper order, as they happened. Use letters only.
    (a) Debbie Allen attends Howard University.
    (b) The movie *Fame* comes out.
    (c) Debbie dances in a revival of *Sweet Charity*.
    (d) Debbie trains the dancers for the TV series *Fame*.

Inferring Tone

18. The tone of Gene Anthony Ray's comment about Debbie (116) is one of **(a)** anger **(b)** annoyance **(c)** respect **(d)** sadness.

Separating Facts from Opinions

For each of the following, tell whether the statement is a fact *(F)* or an opinion *(O)*.

19. Debbie Allen had a part in the movie *Ragtime*.

20. Debbie Allen should not have taken on the extra jobs for the series *Fame*.

Understanding Words from Context

21. She thought it had a good effect. . . . She gave her opinion in this way: "We're doing a show that has a great *impact*, a positive *impact* on people."
Impact (115) means **(a)** effect **(b)** remembrance **(c)** good luck **(d)** insult.

22. "What she preaches is the *perfection* of your art and doing what professionalism dictates that you *must* do."
Perfection (116) means **(a)** study **(b)** a fairly good job **(c)** an excuse for failure **(d)** an excellent job.

23. "What I like about her is her professionalism and how she's always so *straightforward* about everything. . . . She's very tough but very honest at all times."
Straightforward (117) means **(a)** relaxed **(b)** honest **(c)** stubborn **(d)** kindly.

24. During her senior year in high school, she *auditioned* for the North Carolina School of the Arts. The teachers liked her dancing, but rejected her.
Auditioned (118) means **(a)** sang **(b)** wrote **(c)** acted **(d)** tried out.

25. "Dancing is the *loftiest*, the most moving, the most beautiful of the arts."
Loftiest (120) means **(a)** most realistic **(b)** funniest **(c)** highest **(d)** fiercest.

THINKING IT OVER

1. How did Debbie Allen display many talents in the course of her career?
2. How did Debbie's parents play an important role in her success?
3. Why are comments from co-workers so interesting and likely to be true?
4. Did you ever see an episode of *Fame?* Tell about it.
5. Why is it so difficult to earn a living by acting, dancing, or singing?
6. Why do television series demand so much time from the performers?
7. If you had a choice between watching a dance program or a private-eye program, which would you choose? Why?
8. Someone once said, "It's easier to become a success than to remain a success." What does that mean? Do you agree with it?
9. Why do so many television performers fade away after being successful for a time?
10. Do you agree with the statement that "dancing is life itself"? Explain.

ANOTHER LOOK AT THE QUOTATION

> *All that we send into the lives of others*
> *comes back into our own.*
> EDWIN MARKHAM

1. Explain the quotation in your own words.
2. Do you agree with the point of the quotation? Explain.

3. How has Debbie Allen sent good things into the lives of others? How do we know?
4. Have you ever done a good deed without any thought of reward or without anyone's knowing about it? How did you feel? Why did you do it?
5. There's a Balinese saying, "If you are happy, you can always learn to dance." What does this saying mean? Do you agree with it? Explain.

WORDS AT YOUR SERVICE—THE PARTS OF A WORD

> *Her older brother, Tex Allen, is a famous jazz trumpeter and* composer.
> *(118)*

The word *composer* has three parts: *com, pos,* and *er.* The first part, at the beginning of the word, is the *prefix.* Prefixes will be studied more fully on page 145. The second part, in the middle of the word, is the *root.* Roots will be studied more fully on pages 160 and 177. The third part, at the end of the word, is the *suffix.* Suffixes will be studied more fully on page 190.

If you know the parts of an unfamiliar word, you can sometimes guess at the meaning of the word. In the word *composer, com* is a prefix meaning *together. Pos* is a root meaning *put* or *place. Er* is a suffix meaning *one who.* A *composer* is *one who puts things together.* Usually the word is applied to musical creation.

The root usually carries the central meaning. *Pos,* meaning *put* or *place,* appears in other words, like *depose, impose,* and *oppose.*

Not all words have prefixes and suffixes. *Depose, impose,* and *oppose* have prefixes and roots, but no suffixes. *Singer, dancer, selfish,* and *kindness* have roots and suffixes, but no prefixes. A great many words have neither prefixes nor suffixes: *dance, job, deep, show, friend,* and *fun.*

1. In each of the following words, point out the prefix and the root:
   distrust, pretend, reply, report, unsafe
2. In each of the following words, point out the root and the suffix:
   actor, childhood, gently, dancer, actress
3. In each of the following words, point out the prefix, the root, and the suffix:
   concentrate, incredible, replacement, unhappiness, unselfish

COMPLETING AN OUTLINE

The article on Debbie Allen might be outlined in the following way. Five outline items have been omitted. Test your understanding of the structure of the article by following the directions after the outline.

I. *Fame* and Debbie Allen
   A.
   B. Her belief in its message
   C. The show's struggle to survive

II. Debbie's professionalism
   A. Compliment by writer
   B.
   C. Her part in the show's success

III. Early years
    A. Birth in Houston, Texas
    B. Family members
    C. Parents' encouragement
    D.

IV. Growth as dancer
    A. Experiences at Howard University
    B.
    C. Meeting with great dancers

V. Career after college
    A. Broadway roles
    B.
    C. Movie roles
    D. Hopes for *Fame*
    E. A tribute to dancing

Fill in the items omitted from the outline. Correctly match the items in column A with the outline numbers in column B.

A	**B**
1. Encouragement by Mike Malone	**a.** I. A.
2. Disappointment in audition	**b.** II. B.
3. Compliments by cast members	**c.** III. D.
4. Television roles	**d.** IV. B.
5. Debbie's responsibilities on the show	**e.** V. B.

ANOTHER LOOK

HOW MUCH DO YOU REMEMBER?

1. Richard D'Oyly Carte was associated with **(a)** Kareem Abdul-Jabbar **(b)** Debbie Allen **(c)** Martina Navratilova **(d)** Gilbert and Sullivan.

2. Through the years, Martina Navratilova's most frequent opponent has been **(a)** Margaret Court **(b)** Zina Garrison **(c)** Chris Evert Lloyd **(d)** Billie Jean King.

3. Kareem Abdul-Jabbar **(a)** is thought old to play professional basketball **(b)** has never played a game in which he scored less than 25 points **(c)** played his best basketball for the New York Knicks **(d)** never played on a team that beat the Celtics.

4. The TV series that was more successful in England than in the United States is **(a)** *Fame* **(b)** *All in the Family* **(c)** *The Jeffersons* **(d)** *The Cosby Show.*

5. *Utopia Limited* and *The Grand Duke* **(a)** were the first great successes of Gilbert and Sullivan **(b)** have not been as popular as Gilbert and Sullivan's early operettas **(c)** appeared after the death of Arthur Sullivan **(d)** caused a great argument between Gilbert and Sullivan.

6. The person who became an American citizen after leaving her country is (**a**) Chris Evert Lloyd (**b**) Billie Jean King (**c**) Margaret Court (**d**) Martina Navratilova.

7. The team that seemed to hold a jinx over the Lakers is (**a**) the Knicks (**b**) the Celtics (**c**) the Bucks (**d**) UCLA.

8. The person described as *easygoing* is (**a**) W. S. Gilbert (**b**) Martina Navratilova (**c**) Arthur Sullivan (**d**) Debbie Allen.

9. The person who was at one time a lawyer is (**a**) Kareem Abdul-Jabbar (**b**) Chris Evert Lloyd (**c**) W. S. Gilbert (**d**) Richard D'Oyly Carte.

10. At 15 Kareem Abdul-Jabbar was noticeable in a crowd because of his (**a**) height (**b**) weight (**c**) way of dressing (**d**) unusual walk.

WHAT IS YOUR OPINION?

1. Which person or persons in this unit seem to you to have the most interesting life story? Explain.

2. Why are partnerships so difficult? What made the Gilbert and Sullivan partnership especially difficult?

3. What qualities did Martina Navratilova and Kareem Abdul-Jabbar have that brought them to the top?

4. In what way does Debbie Allen resemble Martina or Kareem?

5. What is your favorite sport to watch? To play? Why?

6. Would you rather see a football game on television or go to the game? Explain.

THE QUOTATION AND THE UNIT

> *If you play it safe in life, you've decided*
> *that you don't want to grow anymore.*
>   SHIRLEY HUFSTEDLER

1. Explain the quotation in your own words.
2. Do you agree with the quotation? Explain.
3. Did the subjects in this unit play it safe or take a chance? Explain.
4. How do you accept new challenges? Do you prefer to play it safe or take a chance? Explain.

UNIT 3
WRITERS and ARTISTS

We can do anything we want to do if we stick to it long enough.

HELEN KELLER

Writers and artists help us to understand our world and each other. They show us life through their eyes and guide us to see things we have never noticed before. They reflect the changes in our society and sometimes suggest how we can help create a better world.

The subjects in this unit also entertain or delight us while they instruct us. Arthur Conan Doyle and Agatha Christie brought the detective story to a peak of excellence. They won readers by the millions. They developed fans who read every word, who even formed societies to study their books. They also instructed. The methods of Arthur Conan Doyle's detective, Sherlock Holmes, were adopted by police around the world. Agatha Christie's information about poison once saved a life.

Alice Walker is a different kind of writer. She tells the story of black women in difficulty. She gets inside her subjects' minds and hearts. She makes her characters interesting and sympathetic.

John James Audubon was a man of many talents. He was a naturalist, a writer, and above all a painter of birds. He was the first artist to paint birds that looked real and alive, not stuffed. Today, the nature paintings of others are judged against his.

All four subjects have made important contributions to art and literature.

JOHN JAMES AUDUBON:

Nature's Artist

*We haven't too much time left to ensure
that the government of the earth, by the
earth, and for the earth, shall not perish
[disappear] from the people.*

C. P. SNOW AND PHILIP SNOW

The sky was black with birds. For three days *innumerable* passenger pigeons passed overhead. They were so thick they blotted out the sky. At noon a stranger might have thought there was an eclipse of the sun. The buzzing of the pigeons' wings continued hour after hour.

It was 1813. John James Audubon was traveling to Louisville, Kentucky. The pigeons were migrating, or traveling in flocks. As they neared, Audubon sat down and tried to count the flocks. He put down a dot for each flock, 163 dots in 21 minutes, and then gave up. He couldn't keep up. The number of pigeons increased.

At Louisville the pigeons were thicker than ever. The banks of the Ohio River were filled with men and boys shooting at the flocks above. They killed great numbers, but the pigeon flocks seemed as large as before. Audubon wrote his experiences down in a notebook.

Audubon tried to make an estimate of the number of pigeons in the flocks. He fixed his attention on a column one mile wide, which was below the average size. Then he calculated how many pigeons would pass in three hours. He calculated that there would be more than a billion passenger pigeons in one large flock! If this seems too large, we have the word of another excellent naturalist, Alexander Wilson. He, too, estimated that there might be more than a billion birds in one large flock.

Another authority suggests that in the early 1800s there were probably five billion birds in the three states of Kentucky, Ohio, and Indiana alone. It is hard for us to grasp such a large number of birds today. If we see a flock of a hundred geese, we consider that flock huge. But this number is tiny compared with the average number of passenger pigeons in a flock nearly 200 years ago.

Audubon was convinced that nothing could decrease the number of passenger pigeons except the cutting down of the forests. He was wrong. Less than a century after he made his prediction, the last surviving passenger pigeon died in the Cincinnati Zoo, in 1914.

Like many other species, the passenger pigeon is *extinct*. It has disappeared from the American Midwest. A few stuffed examples and some pictures are all we have to remind us of this once-numerous bird.

How did these birds die out? Some of the forests they depended on were destroyed, but this isn't the whole story. Edward Howe Forbush, another bird authority, suggests that they died out because of the wholesale slaughter of young birds as well as of adults. Since the birds were not nervous or afraid of human beings, they were easily killed. Hunters interfered with their nesting, and the birds could not bring up their young. The numbers dropped from billions to a single bird in a hundred years!

One of the pictures we have of the passenger pigeon is a painting by Audubon. When he roamed the country, the land was still quite unspoiled. His paintings captured the birds of that time. He sometimes preserved pictures of extinct species, birds that had disappeared.

Audubon was born Jean Jacques Audubon, on April 26, 1785. He was the son of a French naval officer stationed in Haiti. When Audubon was a year old, his father returned to France with his family. In France, the young boy lived the life of the wealthy. His father tried to give him a naval education, but the attempt was a failure. His education, though, did give him the artistic skills he would need later in his life's work.

When young Audubon was 18, his father sent him to Mill Grove, near Philadelphia. His father owned property there. In America Audubon changed his name from French *Jean Jacques* to the American *John James*.

In modern slang we'd say, "Audubon was hooked on birds." He watched them and drew them. He had done the same as a teenager in France, but in the United States everything was new to him. The birds were new, beautiful, and everywhere. Audubon was in heaven.

Near his home was a creek. A pair of phoebes lived along the creek. Audubon was enchanted by these birds. At this time he performed a first in American bird study. He tied silver threads about the legs of the young birds. He wanted to see if they came back the following year. Two of the young did. They built their own nests farther up the creek. Audubon was the first American birdbander.

It took a century for birdbanding to take hold on a helpful scale. Nowadays three or four thousand people are permitted to band more than a million birds each year. The United States Fish and Wildlife Service oversees the operation.

Audubon loved the birds, but he also loved a young woman. At Mill Grove he met Lucy Bakewell, a neighbor. When Audubon's father set him up in business in Louisville, Kentucky, Lucy came to visit him. They were married in Louisville.

Lucy is one of the unsung heroes of history. Audubon is justly famous, but he could not have done what he did without his wife. Business wasn't good because of the War of 1812. Gradually, he withdrew from business and spent more time in the fields, studying birds. Often he stayed away months at a time. He earned a poor living as a portrait painter and as a dancing master and fencing instructor.

One of his in-laws once said of Audubon: "He neglects his material interests and is forever wasting his time hunting, drawing, and stuffing birds, and playing the fiddle. We fear he will never be fit for any practical purpose on the face of the earth."

How did the family survive? Another bird artist, Roger Tory Peterson, writes: "During these hand-to-mouth

years, Audubon's devoted wife, Lucy, who had borne two
sons, Victor and John, was both *motive* power and the
balance wheel that kept home and hearth together. She
ran a small private school, taught, and acted from time
to time as a governess, freeing her husband for his creative *endeavors.*" As a governess she took care of children
in a private household.

Audubon's biographer, Francis H. Herrick, also speaks
of Lucy's eagerness to help her husband. Herrick puts
the case even more strongly: "Without her *zeal* and devotion the world would never have heard of Audubon.
His budding talents would have been smothered in some
backwoods town of the Middle West or South."

No one knows when Audubon decided to paint the
native birds and sell the paintings. Perhaps the visit of
another naturalist of the time, Alexander Wilson, gave
him the idea. Wilson was also studying birds. He was
trying to get people to promise to buy his work. Wilson
and Audubon talked about birds and showed each other
their paintings.

Before Audubon came along, others had drawn birds.
But these drawings were stiff. The birds looked stuffed
and not lifelike. As Peterson says, "Audubon took birds
out of the glass cage for all time and gave them the
illusion of life." *Illusion* means that they seemed to be
alive, but they weren't.

In his paintings he made the birds life-size. If the bird's
neck was too long, he'd gracefully droop the head so head
and neck could fit on his page. He painted the birds
against realistic backgrounds. Three of his assistants
painted many of these backgrounds.

Audubon had the idea of publishing his paintings in
an oversize book. He went to Philadelphia and New York,
but no one wanted to risk the money needed for publication.

In 1826, when he was 41, Audubon decided to try

another plan. He took the money he had saved by painting portraits. He added Lucy's savings as a teacher. He sailed to England, hoping to find a printer for his works.

Audubon had caused little excitement in the United States, but in Europe he was a *sensation*. He became an actor of a kind. Though he was used to fine dress in the fine homes of Philadelphia and New Orleans, in Europe he dressed only as an American woodsman. Europeans loved the act. Audubon got his printer.

Audubon got a Scottish engraver to transfer his paintings to the printing plate. The *engraver* is the person who makes prints for printing. The *plate* is the surface from which the printing is done. After only ten plates had been made, the people who added color to the plates went on strike. The strike dragged on for weeks, and Audubon became discouraged.

Finally, Audubon switched to an engraver in London, Robert Havell. Audubon was often lucky in his life. The switch to Havell was an example of his good luck. Havell is considered one of the greatest engravers who ever lived. He sometimes improved the paintings by adding a touch of his own to the plates.

The first printing was called the *Double Elephant Folio*. A *folio* is a large-size book. Audubon bound and distributed about 200 sets. They were priced at $1,000 each. The paintings of Audubon became the model for those that followed him.

What happened to the original paintings from which the prints were made? After Audubon's death, Lucy sold the collection for $4,000. Today the collection is beyond price. In 1863 the New-York Historical Society acquired the collection. In 1985 the collection was put on display for only the third time. Of the 435 original paintings, only two are missing. The paintings of the blue-gray gnatcatcher and the black-throated blue warbler have disappeared. No one knows where.

The original paintings will probably never be sold, but the engraved prints are sold now and then. Prices are out of sight. In January 1985 a single print of the great blue heron sold for $30,800. Remember that this was not the original painting. A full set of 435 prints was sold for $1,716,660. Just 45 years earlier such a set sold for only $14,000.

New prints continue to appear, but even these are expensive. A few of the plates used to make the original prints still exist. You can buy prints from these plates— if you can spare $30,000 for a set of six.

Audubon sparked an interest in birds. In his way, Audubon contributed greatly to the movement to protect the environment. Birds are fragile members of a natural community. When things begin to go wrong in nature, the birds respond to the changes rather quickly. Their actions send out warnings when people have spoiled the environment. For this reason, bird-watchers have led the movement to preserve the environment.

During the last 20 years of his life, Audubon won many honors. That fame has continued. Parks, streets, and towns were named for him. A mountain in Colorado was named for him. In 1905 a bird-protection group, the Audubon Society, was formed. Several United States postage stamps with his portrait and one of his paintings have been issued. On the two-hundredth anniversary of his birth, in 1985, many celebrations were held in his honor. Audubon's work goes on.

UNDERSTANDING WHAT YOU HAVE READ

Finding Another Title

1. Another good title for this selection might be (a) The Origin of the Audubon Society (b) How to Draw Birds from Nature (c) The Man Who Showed Us How to Look at Birds (d) Why Bird Study Helps Preserve Our Environment.

Getting the Main Idea

2. The paintings of John James Audubon (a) showed birds in a realistic, lifelike setting (b) sold for very high amounts in his lifetime (c) have all been lost (d) are not appreciated as much as they ought to be.

Finding Details

3. All of the following states were mentioned as being home for the passenger pigeon EXCEPT (a) Indiana (b) Illinois (c) Kentucky (d) Ohio.
4. The last passenger pigeon died (a) in 1813 (b) in Audubon's lifetime (c) 14 years after Audubon's death (d) in 1914.
5. Audubon was born in (a) France (b) Mill Grove, Pennsylvania (c) Louisville, Kentucky (d) Haiti.
6. The first bird that Audubon studied carefully was the (a) heron (b) blue-gray gnatcatcher (c) phoebe (d) robin.
7. Audubon owed his greatest debt to (a) his son Victor (b) his wife (c) Roger Tory Peterson (d) Francis H. Herrick.

8. Audubon scored a great personal success in **(a)** Europe **(b)** New Orleans **(c)** New York **(d)** Louisville.
9. Robert Havell was **(a)** a writer **(b)** a painter **(c)** an engraver **(d)** a brother-in-law.
10. The first sale of Audubon's collected paintings brought in **(a)** $4,000 **(b)** $14,000 **(c)** $30,000 **(d)** $30,800.

Making Inferences

11. Authorities accept as true the great numbers of passenger pigeons because **(a)** there are photographs showing the large flocks **(b)** both Audubon and Alexander Wilson agreed on the numbers **(c)** Indian legends describe the flight of the passenger pigeon **(d)** there were still large flocks as late as the twentieth century.
12. The purpose of birdbanding is to **(a)** study how birds migrate and how they survive **(b)** follow birds by using radio waves **(c)** provide recreational activities for bird-watchers **(d)** catch specimens for greater convenience in painting.
13. When Audubon took Lucy's savings as a teacher and went to Europe, Lucy was probably **(a)** annoyed **(b)** very angry **(c)** overjoyed **(d)** understanding.
14. Since they were in the same field, between Alexander Wilson and John James Audubon there was probably some **(a)** secret agreement **(b)** feeling of competition **(c)** buying and selling **(d)** discussion of their family problems.
15. In Europe Audubon probably dressed as an American woodsman to **(a)** advertise his book of poetry

(**b**) win for himself a title (**c**) discourage anyone who also had a group of bird paintings (**d**) gain attention.

Predicting What Happens Next

16. If the full set of 435 prints were to be auctioned off in the future, the selling price would probably be (**a**) about $30,000 (**b**) half a million dollars (**c**) more than a million dollars (**d**) less than the price paid in 1985.

Deciding on the Order of Events

17. The following events are scrambled. Arrange them in proper order, as they happened. Use letters only.
    (**a**) Lucy sells the complete collection of paintings.
    (**b**) The New-York Historical Society buys the collection of paintings.
    (**c**) Audubon meets Alexander Wilson.
    (**d**) Audubon comes to Mill Grove, Pennsylvania.

Inferring Tone

18. The tone of the in-law's comments about Audubon (136) is (**a**) admiring (**b**) disrespectful (**c**) comical (**d**) eager.

Separating Facts from Opinions

For each of the following, tell whether the statement is a fact *(F)* or an opinion *(O)*.
19. Audubon's paintings are very much overpriced.
20. A single print of the great blue heron sold for $30,800.

Understanding Words from Context

21. Like many other species, the passenger pigeon is *extinct*. It has disappeared from the American Midwest.
    Extinct (135) means **(a)** widespread **(b)** colorful **(c)** hard to find **(d)** no longer in existence.

22. "During these hand-to-mouth years, Audubon's devoted wife, Lucy, who had borne two sons, Victor and John, was both *motive* power and the balance wheel that kept home and hearth together."
    Motive (136) means **(a)** driving **(b)** unexpected **(c)** weak **(d)** unpleasant.

23. "She ran a private school, taught, and acted from time to time as a governess, freeing her husband for his creative *endeavors*."
    Endeavors (137) means **(a)** wanderings **(b)** paintings **(c)** efforts **(d)** musical abilities.

24. Audubon's biographer, Francis H. Herrick, also speaks of Lucy's eagerness to help her husband. Herrick puts the case even more strongly: "Without her *zeal* and devotion the world would never have heard of Audubon."
    Zeal (137) means **(a)** selfish actions **(b)** constant interruptions **(c)** eager interest **(d)** lazy activities.

25. Audubon had caused little excitement in the United States, but in Europe he was a *sensation*.
    Sensation (138) means a **(a)** singer **(b)** hit **(c)** failure **(d)** printer.

THINKING IT OVER

1. Does it matter whether or not a species dies out forever? Why or why not?

2. Nations around the world have listed what they call their *endangered species:* animals, birds, and plants that are in danger of disappearing. What can be done to keep these species from dying out?

3. What was Audubon's special contribution to bird painting? How did he differ from those who had gone before him?

4. Why does a drop in the number of birds usually warn of something bad in the environment?

5. What part did Lucy Audubon play in her husband's success?

6. Have you ever seen an Audubon bird picture? Tell about your feelings on seeing it.

7. Bird watching is a popular American hobby. What is its appeal?

8. Why did Audubon dress as a backwoodsman when he went to Europe? How do many modern singers try to attract attention to themselves in a similar way?

ANOTHER LOOK AT THE QUOTATION

> We haven't too much time left to ensure that the government of the earth, by the earth, and for the earth, shall not perish [disappear] from the people.
> C. P. SNOW AND PHILIP SNOW

1. This is a switch from the famous quotation by Abraham Lincoln:

> We shall determine "that the government of the people, by the people, and for the people, shall not perish from the earth."

How does the Snow quotation differ from the Lincoln quotation?

2. What warning are the Snows giving?
3. How do people mistreat the earth?
4. What steps can be taken to preserve the environment?

WORDS AT YOUR SERVICE—PREFIXES

For three days innumerable *passenger pigeons passed overhead. (134)*

In the last chapter you learned about the parts of a word: prefixes, roots, and suffixes. In this section, you will concentrate on prefixes. In the sentence above, *innumerable* has a prefix, *in.* If you know the prefix *in,* you have a clue to the meaning of *innumerable. In* means *no, not,* or *without. Innumerable* means *not able to be counted.* Knowing the meaning of the prefix *in* helps you figure out the meanings of many words. The following list contains just a small number of *in* words:

inability—having no skill

inadequate—not enough

inappropriate—not suitable

inattentive—not paying attention

inaudible—not able to be heard

incapable—without skill

incomparable—without an equal

incompetent—lacking ability

incomplete—not finished

inconsistent—not always the same

inconvenient—not convenient

indestructible—not able to be destroyed

indirect—not straight

indistinct—not clear

How many more *in* words can you add?

Here are some other helpful prefixes:

Prefix	Meaning	Example	Definition of the Example Word
com, con	with, together	*com*press	press *together*
de	down	*de*scend	go *down*
non	not, no	*non*believer	someone who doesn't believe
post	after	*post*graduate	*after* graduation
sub	under	*sub*marine	*under* the sea

Fill in the blank in each sentence below by supplying the missing prefix from the list above. The number in parentheses tells you how many letters you need.

EXAMPLE

If something is _____evitable, it is *not* avoidable. (2)
Insert the prefix *in*. The complete word is *inevitable*.

1. If you *press* down a switch, you _____press it. (2)
2. The _____soil is that part of the ground *under* the surface. (3)
3. When people talk *with* each other, they _____municate. (3)
4. If you change a date to a time *after* the original date, you _____pone it. (4)
5. Something that is *not* poisonous is _____toxic. (3)

SIR ARTHUR CONAN DOYLE:

The Real Sherlock Holmes

*The mystery is two stories in one: the
story of what happened and
the story of what appeared to happen.*

MARY ROBERTS RINEHART

To many people, the characters in soap operas are *real*. Fans actually send gifts for a make-believe wedding on a show. They worry if a soap-opera character is ill. They see actors and actresses on the street and address them by their soap-opera names. In a way, their behavior is a tribute to the power television has of making the imaginary seem real.

Sherlock Holmes is a literary character who has earned the same tribute, but with a difference. Soap-opera characters who leave a show are soon forgotten. Sherlock Holmes has been famous for a century. For a hundred years, readers of the Sherlock Holmes stories have believed in his existence. Call someone a "Sherlock Holmes" and nearly everyone understands what you mean. In fact, the fictional character is more famous than the man who created him—Sir Arthur Conan Doyle.

The Holmes story has some strange angles. Sir Arthur Conan Doyle did not consider the Holmes stories his best work. He considered himself a historical novelist first, not a mere detective-story writer. He got tired of Holmes, almost from the start. After he published the successful story, "A Scandal in Bohemia," he gave almost all his time to *The White Company,* a story about knights. *Doyle* may have gotten tired of Holmes, but his readers didn't.

Doyle often thought of "killing off" Holmes. In 1891 he first had the idea of getting rid of Holmes. At that time he needed an idea for the twelfth story in a book, and he was desperate. When he suggested killing off Holmes, his mother said, "You won't! You can't! You mustn't!" She gave him an idea for a story, and he finished the one he had promised.

In a later story he actually had Holmes killed. There were so many objections, though, that he had to bring him back! Holmes stayed with Doyle until a few years before his death.

The creator of Sherlock Holmes was an interesting person in his own right. He was born May 22, 1859, in Edinburgh, Scotland. At Stonyhurst School he was interested in many sports: swimming, cricket, football, hockey, and ice skating. Even as a young man, he showed keen powers of observation.

One subject he didn't care for very much was history. He thought history was too dry, or uninteresting. He preferred his history in fictional form. He preferred the novels of Sir Walter Scott to history books. He carried Scott's novels with him everywhere and once dropped *Ivanhoe,* by mistake, into a stream!

At 15 he visited relatives in London. While there he went to the theater. He enjoyed Madame Tussaud's Wax Museum. It was then located on Baker Street. When years later he gave Sherlock Holmes a London address, he chose 221B Baker Street.

A writer doesn't just create stories out of nothing. Doyle used Baker Street in his detective stories. There were other influences, too. At this time, he read Edgar Allan Poe's great detective story, "The Gold Bug." He was impressed by the clever thinking of the detective, Auguste Dupin.

Writing wasn't Doyle's first choice as a profession. Rather, he decided to become a doctor. At Edinburgh University he studied under Dr. Joseph Bell. Many experts call this man the inspiration for Sherlock Holmes. Dr. Bell stressed the importance of observation in identifying a patient's illness. When his students tried to *diagnose* a disease, Dr. Bell would say, "Use your eyes, ears, hands, and brain. The trained eye! A simple matter!"

Later, Sherlock Holmes, too, would stress over and over again the need to observe carefully.

Doyle didn't expect to make much money as a doctor,

though. To add to his income, he began to write. A story, "The Mystery of Sasassa Valley," was immediately accepted by *Chambers Journal.*

"This is easy!" he thought, and wrote several others. All were *rejected.* Finally another story was accepted: "The American's Tale."

In 1880 he spent seven months as a ship's doctor on an African steamer. He later used his experiences in his writing. In 1881 he got a medical degree, but he needed money to set up a practice.

Meanwhile he had fallen in love with five girls at once. He almost married one of them, Elmo Welden. As his biographer John Dickson Carr wrote, "He was not really in love with Elmo; or she, perhaps, with him. But both were romantic-minded; both thought it an excellent thing to be in love with somebody."

The lovers quarreled all the time. Finally, they broke their relationship. Elmo went to Switzerland. Doyle tried to make a success of his medical practice.

The practice wasn't profitable. Sometimes he wasn't paid. Sometimes he exchanged medical treatment for butter and tea. He kept on writing, with both success and failure. *Cornhill Magazine* bought "Habakuk Jephson's Statement" for a good sum, but most of his other stories were rejected.

At this time one of his patients was Jack Hawkins. The young man had an incurable disease, and there was nothing Doyle could do. Doyle helped the family in every way possible during the young man's illness. By the time of Jack's death, Doyle had fallen in love with Louise Hawkins, Jack's sister. They were married on August 6, 1885.

They were well matched. Louise, or "Touie" as Doyle called her, was unselfish, sympathetic, encouraging—a perfect wife for an energetic man. Doyle turned out many stories during this period of early marriage.

At this time Doyle began to think of Dr. Joseph Bell, his old teacher. "Why not write a detective story using some of the advice given by Dr. Bell?" In 1886 Doyle wrote his first Sherlock Holmes story. *A Study in Scarlet* was a full-length novel. The longer form allowed for a complete introduction to this new detective. At first Doyle thought of calling him "Sherrinford Holmes," but he later settled for "Sherlock Holmes."

Because Doyle was still a practicing physician, he had to steal time to write. He scribbled between calls of the doctor's bell. As John Dickson Carr commented, "He had no idea that he was creating the most famous character in the English language." He was also creating Dr. John Watson, Sherlock Holmes's famous friend and storyteller.

This new novel was not accepted immediately. The person who published *Cornhill Magazine* said it was the wrong length. A second returned it without reading it. A third just said *no*. Finally, a fourth editor gave the book to his wife to read. She said, "This man is a born novelist! It will be a great success."

Unfortunately, the heads of the firm were less enthusiastic. They offered Doyle 25 pounds (about $125) for all rights and said they'd publish the book in a year. Doyle objected, but he finally agreed. And so one of the most famous detective novels in any language was rejected three times and finally sold for a song.

Meanwhile Doyle was writing *Micah Clarke*, a historical novel. This was finally published in 1888. Then in 1890 Doyle wrote another Sherlock Holmes novel, *The Sign of the Four*. Neither this novel nor *A Study in Scarlet* was very successful at first.

Doyle was discouraged. He had little fame and not too much money. He considered becoming an eye surgeon and actually went to Vienna, Austria, to study. His novel of knights and armor, *The White Company*, appeared then—without much public notice.

Sometimes there are clear turning points in a life. We can name a day, a week, or a month and say, "My life changed from that point on." Arthur Conan Doyle's life changed in 1891. By December 1891, six Sherlock Holmes short stories had appeared in print. Unlike Holmes's two novels, they were a hit. Almost overnight the name of Sherlock Holmes was on every reader's lips.

In June 1892 Doyle gave up medicine for a full-time writing career. Here is one of those strange situations that often occur. Like Sir Arthur Sullivan (page 67), Doyle didn't realize that his detective stories showed his true skills. He wanted to write historical novels, not detective stories.

It was after writing two dozen Holmes short stories that Doyle arranged the "death" of Sherlock Holmes. "The Final Problem," published in 1893, has Holmes *supposedly* falling to his death in a Swiss waterfall. There was no proof of death, however. Perhaps in his heart, Doyle thought that Holmes might have to be brought back someday.

The death of Sherlock Holmes caused a public outcry that wouldn't die down. After eight years, Doyle gave in—a little. In 1901–1902 he wrote *The Hound of the Baskervilles.* This was supposed to be about an event that had occurred *before* Holmes's death. Thus he kept up the idea that Holmes was indeed dead.

"More!" the public cried. "We want more."

Doyle gave in. His story "The Adventure of the Empty House" appeared in one magazine in September 1903. It appeared in another magazine a month later. Sherlock Holmes was back. In the story Holmes explains to Watson that he had only pretended to fall into the waterfall. He had spent the following years on secret missions in Tibet and elsewhere.

The public went wild. Booksellers were mobbed. The

magazine *Westminster Gazette* wrote, "That fall over the cliff did not kill Holmes. In fact, he never fell at all. He climbed up the other side of the cliff to escape his enemies and left poor Watson in ignorance. We call this mean. All the same, who can complain?"

Nobody complained. Doyle accepted the public's decision and continued to write Sherlock Holmes stories for the rest of his life. "The Adventure of Shoscombe Old Place" appeared in 1927, only three years before Doyle's death.

Although Doyle was not a trained detective, he developed certain detective practices before anyone else thought of them. Books on detection owe a great deal to him. A pioneering book by Hans Gross, *Criminal Investigation,* appeared in 1891. This was a couple of years after two Holmes novels had been published. A famous head of a police laboratory, Dr. Edmond Locar, once said, "I hold that a police expert, or an examining *magistrate,* would not find it a waste of time to read Doyle's novels."

With his great energy, Doyle created other books. *The Lost World,* in 1911, told of a place where animals of the past still survived. This novel has been produced as well as imitated in the movies.

The Sherlock Holmes stories have been successfully turned into plays and films. In 1899 a play starring William Gillette was very popular. The play, simply titled *Sherlock Holmes,* is often *revived* on the amateur and professional stages. Many actors have tried their hand at Sherlock Holmes in the movies, too. Perhaps the most famous of all is Basil Rathbone, who played Holmes in a great many movies. A recent series of plays on television featured Jeremy Brett as the detective. Sherlock Holmes will probably go on as long as people like a good mystery with a fascinating detective.

Doyle's life was exciting in other ways too. He was a

leader, in the forefront of many good causes. He was a doctor in the South African Boer War in 1900. He warned of the danger of submarines long before World War I. He suggested building a tunnel underneath the English Channel, from France to England. He spoke against colonial cruelty in the Belgian Congo, now Zaire. He helped fight for two persons he felt had been wrongfully convicted of a crime.

His first wife died after a long illness. Doyle stayed with her till the end. He married a second time, in 1907. Jean Leckie Doyle proved to be a friend and supporter through his final years.

His son Kingsley, who was wounded in 1916 in France, died of the flu in 1918. Doyle became interested in communicating with the dead and spent his later years talking on this subject. When he died in 1930, the world mourned him.

UNDERSTANDING WHAT YOU HAVE READ

Finding Another Title

1. Another good title for this selection might be **(a)** How to Write a Good Detective Story **(b)** The Beginning of Detective Fiction in the United States **(c)** Sherlock Holmes and the Man Who Created Him **(d)** Sherlock Holmes and the Movies.

Getting the Main Idea

2. Arthur Conan Doyle **(a)** wrote good novels about knights **(b)** had several tragedies in his life **(c)** wrote detective stories under different names **(d)** was a man of many talents.

Finding Details

3. At school Doyle took part in all the following sports EXCEPT **(a)** swimming **(b)** track **(c)** football **(d)** hockey.

4. Doyle's story about knights is called **(a)** "A Scandal in Bohemia" **(b)** *The White Company* **(c)** "The American's Tale" **(d)** *A Study in Scarlet.*

5. The doctor who taught Doyle to observe carefully was **(a)** Joseph Bell **(b)** John Dickson Carr **(c)** Jack Hawkins **(d)** Arthur Sullivan.

6. The person who objected strongly to the idea of "killing off" Holmes was **(a)** Louisa Hawkins Doyle **(b)** Holmes's father **(c)** Holmes's mother **(d)** the editor of *Cornhill Magazine.*

7. Auguste Dupin appears in the famous story called **(a)** "The Mystery of Sasassa Valley" **(b)** "Habakuk Jephson's Statement" **(c)** "The Final Problem" **(d)** "The Gold Bug."

8. Elmo Welden was **(a)** a person Doyle almost married **(b)** a shipmate of Doyle's **(c)** a fellow doctor at medical school **(d)** an editor.

9. The year that was a turning point in Doyle's writing career was **(a)** 1880 **(b)** 1887 **(c)** 1891 **(d)** 1900.

10. Jean Leckie **(a)** went to school with Doyle **(b)** was a Scottish aunt **(c)** was a writer of historical novels **(d)** was Doyle's second wife.

Making Inferences

11. Sherlock Holmes is probably so well loved because he **(a)** seems so real **(b)** never gets angry **(c)** makes fun of his assistant Watson **(d)** tells humorous stories.

12. Doyle wrote his first Sherlock Holmes novel to (a) please his wife (b) make money (c) do better than Edgar Allan Poe (d) amuse himself during a cold winter.
13. Probably Doyle (a) did not understand his fans' love for Sherlock Holmes (b) was a slow writer who had few things published (c) did not understand the role of submarines in modern warfare (d) enjoyed poetry but did not enjoy reading novels.
14. In writing about crime and crime detection, Doyle was (a) a good observer but a poor writer (b) often careless with facts (c) ahead of his time (d) too much influenced by his wife.
15. Because Doyle was a doctor, he probably (a) continued to practice actively his entire life (b) treated all his friends without charge (c) made Sherlock Holmes a doctor, too (d) used his knowledge of medicine to write his stories.

Predicting What Happens Next

16. In the years ahead, Sherlock Holmes stories will probably (a) be rewritten by another writer (b) continue to be very popular (c) be used for the movies but not for television (d) die out quickly.

Deciding on the Order of Events

17. The following events are scrambled. Arrange them in proper order, as they happened. Use letters only.
    (a) *The Sign of the Four* is published.
    (b) Doyle attends Stonyhurst School.
    (c) Doyle attends Edinburgh University.
    (d) *A Study in Scarlet* is published.

Inferring Attitude

18. When Dr. Joseph Bell told his students to use their eyes (149), he was probably **(a)** covering up his real views **(b)** being serious and direct **(c)** trying to tell a joke **(d)** forgetting more important things.

Separating Facts from Opinions

For each of the following, tell whether the statement is a fact *(F)* or an opinion *(O)*.

19. Doyle should have stuck to writing historical novels.

20. Doyle wrote several historical novels.

Understanding Words from Context

21. Dr. Bell stressed the importance of observation in identifying a patient's illness. When his students tried to *diagnose* a disease, Dr. Bell would say, "Use your eyes, ears, hands, and brain."
Diagnose (149) means **(a)** cure **(b)** identify **(c)** overlook **(d)** cause.

22. "The Final Problem," published in 1893, has Holmes *supposedly* falling to his death in a Swiss waterfall. There was no proof of death, however.
Supposedly (152) means **(a)** really **(b)** sadly and finally **(c)** believed to be true **(d)** carelessly and foolishly.

23. "I hold that a police expert, or an examining *magistrate,* would not find it a waste of time to read Doyle's novels."
A *magistrate* (153) is a **(a)** newspaper reporter **(b)** teacher **(c)** judge **(d)** criminal.

24. In 1899 a play starring William Gillette was very popular. The play, simply titled *Sherlock Holmes,* is often *revived* on the amateur and professional stages.

Revived (153) means **(a)** neglected **(b)** photographed **(c)** taped **(d)** brought back.

25. He was a leader, in the *forefront* of many good causes.

Forefront (154) means **(a)** position of importance **(b)** committee meeting **(c)** middle position **(d)** opposition.

THINKING IT OVER

1. Why did Arthur Conan Doyle finally give up his medical practice? Was he wise to do so? Explain.
2. When a television star asks to drop out of a television series, his or her part is "written out." The character may be "killed" or sent away to another city. If there is a chance the star may want to return to the series someday, what do the series writers do? Why?
3. How was it possible for Doyle to "bring back to life" the supposedly dead detective? How is this similar to what happens on television programs?
4. How did Doyle's experiences show that a writer's life is not easy? What disappointments did he face?
5. John Dickson Carr wrote of Doyle's love affair: "He was not really in love with Elmo; or she, perhaps, with him. But both were romantic-minded; both thought it an excellent thing to be in love with somebody." How is being "romantic-minded" different from loving someone? How would you explain what was wrong with the lovers' relationship?

6. How did Dr. Joseph Bell play an important part in the development of Sherlock Holmes?
7. What is the difference between *looking* and *observing?* Which requires more thought?
8. Have you ever read a Sherlock Holmes story or seen one on television? Tell about it.
9. Why did Doyle give in and write Holmes stories almost until his death?
10. Sherlock Holmes stressed reason, or logic, over emotions. What other characters in literature or on television are logical rather than emotional? Tell about them.

ANOTHER LOOK AT THE QUOTATION

> *The mystery is two stories in one: the story of what happened and the story of what appeared to happen.*
> MARY ROBERTS RINEHART

1. Explain the quotation in your own words.
2. The phrase *mystery story* is a broad term. It includes the detective story and other types of stories as well. In her quotation, Mary Roberts Rinehart is probably thinking especially of the detective story. A good detective story presents a puzzle. It provides the clues to its solution; then the detective shows how the clues point out the murderer. A good detective-story writer tries to keep readers guessing. Why do we enjoy puzzles and riddles? Why do we like a detective story that plays fair and still puzzles us?
3. Every story has characters, setting, and a plot, or plan of the story. Which of these three do you think is most important in a detective story? Why?

WORDS AT YOUR SERVICE—LATIN ROOTS

> *"This is easy!"* he thought and wrote
> many others. All were rejected. *Finally*
> *another story was accepted:* "The Amer-
> *ican's Tale."* (150)

The contrast of *accepted* and *rejected* tells you that *re-jected* means the opposite of *accepted*. But there is an-other clue to the meaning of *rejected*. The root *ject* turns up again and again in English. A serum is *injected* into the bloodstream. Pictures are *projected* onto a screen. The root *ject* means *cast* or *throw*.

When you uncover this meaning, you have clues to other words formed from this root. If you are *dejected,* you are *cast* down. A disturbing person may be *ejected* (*cast* out) from a meeting. An *interjection* is a word, like *ouch!*, that is *cast* into a sentence to show emotion. A person who makes an *objection throws* something into the way of another's ideas. Knowing a few of these help-ful roots will enlarge your vocabulary.

Here are five additional Latin roots:

Root	Meaning	Example	Definition of the Example Word
ag, act	act, do, drive	*ag*ent	one who *acts* for another
ced, ceed	go, yield	ex*ceed*	*go* beyond
dic, dict	say, speak	pre*dict*	*speak* in advance
fac, fy	make, do	magni*fy*	*make* large
pon, pos	place, put	com*pose*	*put* together

Fill in the blank in each sentence below by supplying the missing root from the list above. The number in parentheses tells you how many letters you need.

EXAMPLE

People in sub_____ion have been *cast* down, put under the rule of others. (4)

Insert the root *ject*. The complete word is *subjection*.

1. If flood waters *go* back, they are said to re_____e. (3)
2. A _____tory is a place where workers *make* various products. (3)
3. If we post_____e a date, we *put* the new date later than the old one. (3)
4. The _____enda is a list of things that the members must *do* during a meeting. (2)
5. A _____ionary is a book that contains the words people *speak* and write. (4)

AGATHA CHRISTIE:
Queen of the Whodunits

*Make 'em laugh; make 'em cry; make
'em wait.*

CHARLES READE

The little girl was dying. There was no doubt. The doctors had tried everything they knew. There was no improvement. The child kept getting worse and worse. Just about everyone had given up hope.

Nurse Maitland sat by the little girl. To pass the time, she read a mystery story. It was called *The Pale Horse,* by Agatha Christie. Suddenly the nurse gave a gasp of excitement.

The murderer in the novel had tried out a rare poison. This substance, called *thallium,* may be used for making *photoelectric* cells, rat poison, and other products. It was also used for murder in Agatha Christie's detective story.

The description of the victim's symptoms in the novel matched those of the little girl. Children often put things in their mouths. Could the little girl have swallowed some of this poisonous substance?

Nurse Maitland dropped the book and rushed to the doctor on the case. The doctor had been puzzled about the cause of the girl's illness. Now he tried a new line of treatment. The treatment was successful, and the little girl's life was saved.

Detective stories are usually read for pure entertainment. This was one detective story that actually saved a life. The author of *The Pale Horse* is the world's most famous woman writer of mystery stories.

Agatha Christie was born Agatha Mary Clarissa Miller on September 15, 1891, in Devonshire, England. Her father was Frederick Miller, an American who had come to live in England. He married an Englishwoman and settled in a quiet town on the coast. Just after Agatha's eleventh birthday, her father died at the age of 55. Her mother became totally responsible for raising young Agatha.

Apparently Mrs. Miller had unusual ideas about education. Agatha's elder sister had gone away to school.

When Agatha's turn came, her mother decided to keep her at home. Agatha's education was not neglected, however. Many people came to her home to teach her. She also went out to all kinds of classes. She attended classes in art, singing, piano, cooking, and exercise.

Agatha was bright. She had taught herself to read when she was only three. After her father's death, a bad cold kept her indoors. Her mother suggested she write a story. Agatha was only 11 years old.

Derrick Murdoch, a biographer of Agatha Christie, wrote: "In one of her interviews in later years, Agatha said that her mother was a remarkable woman who taught her to believe she could accomplish anything she set her mind to do. So, just as simply as that, she started writing."

Much of her early writing was not very good. She might have become discouraged, but she had a famous neighbor who encouraged her. At that time Eden Phillpotts, the neighbor, was a leading writer of novels and detective stories. His influence on Agatha changed her life.

When Agatha was 16, her mother had another idea altogether. She sent Agatha to Paris to study music and voice training. Agatha was a fine musician, but she was too shy. When she performed on the piano before a group, she lost her confidence. She sang well but not well enough for a career as a concert soprano.

Mrs. Miller called Agatha back from Paris to get ready for the social season. At that time, mothers carefully mapped out their strategy. Since careers for women were so limited, mothers planned ways to make good marriages for their daughters. They gave dances, picnics, and parties. Somewhere, somehow, they'd find suitable husbands for their daughters.

Was Agatha likely to find a handsome young man? As

Derrick Murdoch wrote, "Agatha was a tall, well-built and striking-looking young lady who could dance, play the piano exceptionally well, sing charmingly, and had excellent party manners. If she was a shy conversationalist, many men would not see that as a disadvantage."

The last sentence says a great deal about men's view of women at that time.

Mrs. Miller's strategy worked. At 22, Agatha was engaged to a handsome young man just a year older than she. Lieutenant Archibald Christie was admired by every young woman in the area. He was considered a good catch, and Agatha's future looked bright.

Agatha and Archibald were married on Christmas Eve in 1914. World War I had broken out the previous August, and Captain Archibald Christie went off to war. He spent most of the war years in France and had a *distinguished* record. He was mentioned five times in reports and was awarded a number of medals. When the war ended, he was a lieutenant colonel.

Under her married name, Agatha Christie had a detective novel published in 1920. She followed *The Mysterious Affair at Styles* with other novels fairly quickly. The money from these detective stories helped give Agatha and her husband financial independence.

In 1922 Agatha and Archibald Christie traveled around the world to provide publicity for the British Empire Exhibition. For a while it seemed like a perfect marriage. The attractive young wife and her handsome army officer seemed happy.

This happy picture was not true. No one knows the entire story. Archibald Christie had fallen in love with a younger woman, Nancy Neele. There were attempts to save the failing marriage, but Agatha and Archibald Christie were divorced in 1928. Agatha won custody of their child, but she had lost a great deal.

Two years before the divorce, Agatha had a strange experience. The year 1926 was a curious one in our tale of Agatha Christie. In that year she published *The Murder of Roger Ackroyd*. This is one of the most unusual detective stories ever written. It has a plot twist at the end that startles everyone. It drew sharp attacks. Many critics said she had not played by the rules. But others called the book one of the greatest detective stories of all time.

Agatha was upset by the unfavorable reviews. She was also troubled by her failing marriage. Then something happened that has remained a mystery to this day.

On December 3, 1926, she got into her car, drove away from home, and vanished. Someone discovered her abandoned car the next morning. She had left her fur coat on the seat. She had left the lights in the *on* position, so the batteries were dead.

The police feared the worst. Thousands of police and volunteers searched the area. Divers explored a nearby lake. There was no sign of Agatha Christie. She had disappeared completely. The mystery writer became part of a real-life mystery that no one could solve.

On the eleventh day, newspaper headlines announced that Agatha Christie had been found. More than a week earlier she had checked into a hotel under the name of Teresa Neele of South Africa. She was friendly, *mingling* with other guests, and at first aroused no suspicion. Then one of the employees noticed the resemblance between "Teresa Neele" and the description of the missing Agatha Christie. Her husband was called. He went to the hotel and found his wife.

Why had she run away? Had she suffered a nervous breakdown? Agatha Christie always refused to discuss this episode. Many explanations have been offered. A recent movie, for example, showed her in love with another man during these missing days. Some people called it a publicity stunt. No one really knows.

A few things are certain. Doctors examined Agatha and said she had suffered from amnesia, or loss of memory. What had caused amnesia, if this is truly the explanation? There are three possible causes. First, her mother had died that year. Second, her book *The Murder of Roger Ackroyd* had been attacked bitterly. Third, her marriage was failing. It may not be surprising that she took the last name of Nancy Neele, the woman her husband would later marry.

Fate had been unkind to Agatha, but her life would soon change for the better. In one of her trips abroad she met a young man, Max Mallowan. He was an archeologist, a person who digs in the ruins of ancient cities and studies lost civilizations. Max was working on uncovering an ancient city. Max was 14 years younger than Agatha, but they fell in love. They were married in September 1930, just before Agatha's fortieth birthday. This marriage lasted happily till her death.

For the rest of her life Agatha traveled with Max all over the world. She used many of her experiences in detective stories, with titles like *Death on the Nile* and *Murder in Mesopotamia.* Because she had made her reputation with the name of *Christie,* she kept it professionally.

What makes Agatha Christie so popular? She is not considered a great writer. Most of her characters have only a few special characteristics. In her early novels she shows some of the narrow-minded *prejudices* of her social class. She has been called a snob. She seemed to believe that she and her friends were superior to the average run of people. She had little sense of humor.

Most of her novels of the 1920s are thrillers, not true detective stories. They are exaggerated and filled with unlikely action. A true detective story presents a puzzle. The writer gives the readers all the clues. The reader can match wits with the detective. The person who solves the crime, the sleuth, may be a professional police officer, a private investigator, or an ordinary citizen. (As we have seen in the Sherlock Holmes stories, Holmes is an amateur, not a professional.) If Christie had written only these thrillers, her reputation would not have been lasting.

In the 1930s Agatha Christie began to develop her creative talents. After her marriage to Max Mallowan, the level of her stories rose. They were better plotted and more readable. They were true detective stories. When she returned to thrillers, she usually failed.

Why has she remained so popular? She has created two immortal detectives. Her Belgian detective, Hercule Poirot, appeared in more of her stories than any other. But Miss Marple, quiet resident of St. Mary Mead, is a popular figure in many others.

Perhaps the most important reason for her success is that she is easy and fun to read. But the reader must pay attention. She creates puzzles that the detective solves at the end. The reader has all the clues and should be able to guess who the criminal is. But Christie is very sly. She can cleverly mislead the reader. At the end most readers say, "That's great! I should have discovered that myself!"

In the book *A Talent to Deceive,* the writer Robert Barnard discusses a typical Christie novel. He points out that a good Christie tale has a carefully thought-out plot. Every detail is important and in its proper place. "Above all, the reader has that satisfying sense that the clues have all been fairly and squarely placed in front of him— even if he has somehow been induced [forced] to look out of the window at the *crucial* moment of placing."

Agatha tried to write a novel for Christmas each year. During 50 years of writing, her output was unbelievable. A list published in Derrick Murdoch's *The Agatha Christie Mystery* shows 94 different titles! Not all are up to her high standards, but a surprising number are very readable today.

Throughout the world hers are the best-selling books after the Bible and Shakespeare.

Hercule Poirot remained Agatha Christie's best-known detective. But Agatha Christie at times tired of her own creation. She had produced ten Poirot books in four years. She decided to kill off Poirot in a book titled *Curtain*. She wrote the book during World War II and probably intended this to be the last Poirot book. But her public demanded more Poirot books, just as Arthur Conan Doyle's public demanded more Sherlock Holmes books. She did write more Poirot books, but she hid *Curtain* away and instructed that it be published after her death.

In 1975 she realized she could not produce her usual "Christmas book." She allowed the editors to take *Curtain* from the vault and publish it. Readers were sad to learn of the death of their beloved detective. A few months later, on the morning of January 12, 1976, Poirot's creator was dead.

No report on Agatha Christie would be complete without a look at other forms of entertainment based on her writing. Agatha Christie's popularity goes far beyond the books themselves. She has been a favorite in the movies, on television, and on stage.

As long ago as 1928 two movies were based on stories by Agatha Christie. In the 1930s four films using her stories were produced. Her film popularity continued throughout the rest of her life. One of the most successful of all films was *Witness for the Prosecution* in 1957. It starred Tyrone Power, Marlene Dietrich, Charles Laughton, and Elsa Lanchester. Its ending is one of the most surprising in movie history.

Her famous detective, Hercule Poirot, has been played by the major film stars Albert Finney, Tony Randall, and Peter Ustinov. Angela Lansbury and Margaret Rutherford have played Miss Marple.

Television has often used Christie's stories. Helen Hayes has played Miss Marple. A number of other Christie stories without Poirot or Miss Marple have been successful on television.

Perhaps Christie's greatest triumph has come on the stage. She herself wrote several plays. One of them, *Black Coffee,* featured Francis L. Sullivan as Poirot. *The Murder of Roger Ackroyd* was put on the London stage in 1928 with Charles Laughton as Poirot.

An amusing musical comedy, *Something's Afoot,* is based on one of Agatha's cleverest stories. It had a successful Broadway run. Since then it has been performed around the country. It has pleased audiences in dinner theaters, on school stages, and in summer theaters. The name *Agatha Christie* is magic.

We have spoken about one success after another, but we have not yet mentioned the most amazing one of all. In 1947 Agatha wrote a radio play, *Three Blind Mice.* She decided to expand the radio play to a full-length stage play. She called it *The Mousetrap.* It opened in London on November 25, 1952. It got pleasant reviews, but no one could foresee the future.

In 1954 the play began to lose money for the first time. It was about to close when ticket sales suddenly increased. American tourists decided they just had to see the play. It continued to run. In its twenty-first year the play was transferred to a larger theater.

The Mousetrap kept going on and on without a break.

It set new world's records for *consecutive* performances. On the night of Agatha Christie's death, *The Mousetrap* was giving its 9,612th performance.

As you read this, the play may still be running.

UNDERSTANDING WHAT YOU HAVE READ

Finding Another Title

1. Another good title for this selection might be (a) A Master of the Detective Story (b) The Personal Life of Agatha Christie (c) Agatha Christie's Success in the Movies (d) Agatha Christie Saves a Life.

Getting the Main Idea

2. Agatha Christie (a) was sometimes wrong in her attitudes (b) never wrote a bad book (c) earned her fame over a long period (d) disappeared mysteriously for 11 days.

Finding Details

3. A person who encouraged Agatha in her early writing was (a) Derrick Murdoch (b) her singing teacher (c) her father (d) Eden Phillpotts.
4. Agatha and Archibald Christie were married (a) immediately after their engagement was announced. (b) a few months after the outbreak of World War I (c) in France (d) at the end of World War I.

5. The first Christie novel to be published was **(a)** *The Pale Horse* **(b)** *The Mysterious Affair at Styles* **(c)** *The Murder of Roger Ackroyd* **(d)** not mentioned in the selection.

6. Agatha Christie disappeared for more than a week in **(a)** 1914 **(b)** 1918 **(c)** 1920 **(d)** 1926.

7. All the following are suggested as a possible reason for Agatha Christie's amnesia EXCEPT **(a)** a disagreement with her book company **(b)** the death of her mother **(c)** bad reviews **(d)** trouble with her marriage.

8. Robert Barnard and Derrick Murdoch are both **(a)** actors **(b)** athletes **(c)** writers **(d)** editors.

9. Which of the following statements may accurately be made about *Curtain?*
   (a) It was written near the time of Agatha Christie's death.
   (b) It tells of the death of Hercule Poirot.
   (c) It was Agatha Christie's most successful novel.
   (d) It was published during World War II.

10. All the following are mentioned as having played Miss Marple EXCEPT **(a)** Angela Lansbury **(b)** Helen Hayes **(c)** Margaret Rutherford **(d)** Agatha Christie herself.

Making Inferences

11. "If she was a shy conversationalist, many men would not see that as a disadvantage." (164)
    This quotation tells us that men probably **(a)** wanted to marry only beautiful women **(b)** would not have liked Agatha Christie **(c)** liked quiet, bashful women **(d)** liked to please the mothers of the girls they courted.

12. Agatha Christie probably wrote *Murder in Mesopotamia* **(a)** after a visit to that area with her husband **(b)** to prove she could write a good novel without Hercule Poirot **(c)** a year after *The Mysterious Affair at Styles* **(d)** near the end of her life.

13. If Agatha had made her name famous for the first time after her second marriage, she would probably have **(a)** written under her maiden name, Agatha Miller **(b)** called herself *Agatha Mallowan* **(c)** written only detective stories, not thrillers **(d)** signed movie contracts much earlier.

14. The description of Agatha Christie's novels of the 1920s suggests that they are **(a)** not as good as those of the 1930s **(b)** the best detective stories of her career **(c)** all detective stories, not thrillers **(d)** read by students of medicine for medical assistance.

15. Movie and television producers are eager to present shows based on stories by Agatha Christie because **(a)** the producers are personal friends of the author **(b)** the shows automatically guarantee a fortune for the companies **(c)** Agatha Christie is so popular with audiences **(d)** the shows all contain the character of Hercule Poirot.

Predicting What Happens Next

16. Within the next few years there will probably be **(a)** a loss of popularity for the Agatha Christie books **(b)** a claim that Agatha Christie stole her best ideas from other authors **(c)** a solution to Agatha's disappearance of 1926 **(d)** at least one TV or film production of an Agatha Christie book.

Deciding on the Order of Events

17. The following events are scrambled. Arrange them in proper order, as they happened. Use letters only.
    (a) Agatha Christie marries Max Mallowan.
    (b) Frederick Miller dies.
    (c) Agatha Christie allows the novel *Curtain* to be published.
    (d) Agatha Miller marries Archibald Christie.

Inferring Tone

18. In his comment on the writing of Agatha Christie (168), Robert Barnard is (a) admiring (b) scornful (c) undecided (d) irritated.

Separating Facts from Opinions

For each of the following, tell whether the statement is a fact (*F*) or an opinion (*O*).

19. Miss Marple is really a much more interesting detective than Hercule Poirot.

20. Agatha Christie wrote *The Murder of Roger Ackroyd* after *The Mysterious Affair at Styles*.

Understanding Words from Context

21. He spent most of the war years in France and had a *distinguished* record. He was mentioned five times in reports and was awarded a number of medals.
    Distinguished (165) means (a) poor (b) impossible (c) better than anyone else's (d) marked by honor.

22. She was friendly, *mingling* with other guests, and at first aroused no suspicion.

Mingling (166) means **(a)** arguing **(b)** going swimming **(c)** mixing **(d)** singing and dancing.

23. In her early novels she shows some of the narrow-minded *prejudices* of her social class. She has been called a snob.

    Prejudices (167) are **(a)** unfair judgments made in advance **(b)** strange habits of behavior **(c)** funny ways of acting in public **(d)** kind and generous actions.

24. "Above all, the reader has that satisfying sense that the clues have all been fairly and squarely placed in front of him—even if he has somehow been *induced* [forced] to look out the window at the *crucial* moment of placing."

    Crucial (168) means **(a)** humorous **(b)** important **(c)** boring **(d)** sad.

25. *The Mousetrap* kept going on and on without a break. It has set new world's records for *consecutive* performances.

    Consecutive (171) means **(a)** entertaining **(b)** without interruption **(c)** light **(d)** with a feeling of excitement.

THINKING IT OVER

1. Do you enjoy reading detective stories? Tell why or why not.

2. There are many detective stories on television. Some, like *Murder, She Wrote,* with Angela Lansbury, are similar to those of Agatha Christie. The main interest is the puzzle. Viewers try to figure out who killed the victim. Why are shows like these popular?

3. Then there are the hardboiled detectives like Mike Hammer and Hunter. Clint Eastwood's Dirty Harry, in the movies, is also this kind of detective. Which type of detective story do you like better? Explain.

4. How did the education of women in Agatha Christie's day differ from the education of women today? Use your library for help in answering the question.

5. How did Agatha Christie's upbringing at first help make her a narrow-minded snob? Why do you think she began to lose her prejudices?

6. Why are people prejudiced against other groups? What part does ignorance play in prejudice? How can prejudices be removed?

7. Although she was raised as a quiet girl, Agatha Christie created something new in her books—a successful woman detective. Which of her characters showed that women have the same abilities as men? What effect might such a character have on readers?

8. Agatha Christie's books are eagerly read by people all over the world. What do *you* look for in your reading? What makes you decide to read a particular book or magazine?

9. Perhaps you have seen a rerun of *Death on the Nile, The Mirror Cracked,* or another Christie story in the movies or on television. Tell about it.

10. A new biography of Agatha Christie appeared in 1985. What does its appearance suggest about her popularity?

ANOTHER LOOK AT THE QUOTATION

Make 'em laugh; make 'em cry; make 'em wait.

CHARLES READE

1. The quotation is Charles Reade's recipe for a successful novel. What, according to Reade, are the three necessary ingredients?
2. Which of these three ingredients is most important in a detective story? Why?
3. Do you enjoy a story with all three ingredients? Explain.
4. Some movies are called *tear-jerkers*. They are rated *one-handkerchief movies* or *two-handkerchief movies* and so on. Why do people actually enjoy crying at a movie?
5. Another word for "make 'em wait" is *suspense*. Tell about a movie or television show you've seen and show how it used suspense to keep the audience interested.

WORDS AT YOUR SERVICE—GREEK ROOTS

> *This substance, called* thallium, *may be used for making* photoelectric *cells and other products. (163)*

Even if the word *photoelectric* is new to you, the root *photo* is familiar. You probably know the words *photo, photograph,* and *telephoto* lens. You may be aware that the root has something to do with *light*. You decide that a *photoelectric* cell is controlled by a beam of light. *Photoelectric* cells can open doors or set off burglar alarms. You may recall the expression *electric eye*, which means the same as *photoelectric cell*.

Knowing a few familiar Greek roots can help build your vocabulary. Here are five additional, helpful Greek roots:

Root	Meaning	Example	Definition of the Example Word
astr, aster	star	*aster*isk	a *star*-shaped symbol (*)
auto	self	*auto*graph	signature written by one*self*
dyn	power	*dyn*amic	full of energy, *power*ful
ge	earth	*ge*ology	study of the *earth*
therm	heat	*therm*al	pertaining to *heat*

Fill in the blank in each sentence below by supplying the missing root from the list above. The number in parentheses tells you how many letters you need.

EXAMPLE

In the process of _____synthesis, plants use sun*light* to create chlorophyll. (5)

Insert the root *photo*. The complete word is *photosynthesis*.

1. A branch of knowledge that began with the measurement of the *earth* is called _____ometry. (2)
2. A common device for measuring *heat* is the _____ometer. (5)
3. The scientific study of *stars* is called _____onomy. (4)
4. A *powerful* explosive is known as _____amite. (3)
5. A device that works by it*self* is _____matic. (4)

ALICE WALKER:
Prize-Winning Writer

*Those who try to do something and fail
are infinitely better than those who try
to do nothing and succeed.*

RICHARD BIRD

There is an old expression that the acorn doesn't fall far from the tree. We all resemble our mothers and fathers in some ways, often in unexpected ways. We are influenced by the teachings and actions of our parents. Alice Walker is a famous poet, novelist, and writer of short stories and essays. She admits her debt to her parents.

In an interview with Jacqueline Trescott of the *Washington Post,* Alice said, "I grew up believing that there was nothing . . . my mother couldn't do once she set her mind to it." She paused a moment and then added, "So in a way when the . . . women's movement happened, I was really delighted because I felt they were trying to go where my mother was and where I always assumed I would go."

Both of Alice Walker's parents were storytellers. Alice was only eight when she began to write down some of these stories. At that time she also began writing poetry. Because conditions were crowded at home, she used to write outdoors. She would roam the fields and find a quiet spot to think and write.

Alice was born on February 8, 1944, in Eatonton, Georgia. She was the youngest of eight children. The family was poor but was rich in love.

In 1952 an accident changed her outlook on life. One of her brothers accidentally shot Alice in the eye with a BB gun. She lost the sight of one eye. A layer of scar tissue formed over the eye, and she became very shy. Some of her classmates made fun of her. Even the kind ones stared at her. This experience caused her to withdraw from people. She started to read and write poetry.

Fortunately, when Alice was 14, an operation removed the ugly scar tissue. She did not regain the sight of the eye, but it no longer looked unpleasant. Sometimes we benefit in strange ways by misfortune. Alice said that as a result of the accident, she began "really to see people and things, really to notice relationships and to learn to be patient enough to care about how they turned out."

She was the outstanding student in her graduating class. Her fellow students voted her most popular and queen of the senior class. She also won a scholarship to Spelman College in Atlanta beginning in 1961.

At this time Alice became interested in the civil-rights movement. Because of problems at Spelman, she transferred to Sarah Lawrence College in Bronxville, New York. In 1964 she traveled to Africa.

During this time she wrote a great deal of poetry. The poetry showed her deepest interests and concerns. Two major topics were Africa and the civil-rights movement. At the college she slipped her poems under the door of her teacher, Muriel Rukeyser.

Muriel Rukeyser was herself a well-known poet. When she read Alice's poems, she was impressed. As a famous poet, she had an agent, or business manager. She showed Alice's poems to the agent. He gave them to Hiram Haydn, an editor for a major book company. Alice's collection of poems, *Once,* was published in 1969. A reviewer in the magazine *Poetry,* Lisel Mueller, praised the poems highly. She called the young author "sensitive, spirited, and intelligent." She praised her "wit and tenderness."

Alice graduated from Sarah Lawrence College in 1965. She kept writing and won a writing fellowship in 1966. A *fellowship* meant that for the first time she would be paid while she was writing.

She continued her active role in the civil-rights movement. She met and married Melvyn Leventhal, a civil-rights lawyer. During this time her first essay was published. Shortly after, she won the $300 first prize in the annual essay contest of the *American Scholar.*

In September 1967 the Leventhals moved to Mississippi. While there, Alice became a black-history expert for a Head Start program. She was also a writer-in-residence at Jackson State College and Tougaloo College. Along with these jobs, she continued to write.

She completed her first novel, *The Third Life of Grange Copeland,* while on fellowship at a writers' colony in New Hampshire. The book was published in 1970. Although the reviews were mixed, the reviewers realized that a new talent had arrived. Alice's novels deal with difficult problems. They are not children's books but are intended for mature readers.

Alice was asked to lecture at both Wellesley College and the University of Massachusetts in 1972–1973. To be near her work, she moved to Massachusetts. She stayed a year and a half.

These were difficult times for the young author. Because of her work, she had to be away from her husband. In 1973 her father died. Still, Alice kept writing. This was her way of dealing with harsh blows of reality.

In 1973 three more of her books were published. One was a book of poetry. A second was a collection of her short stories. The third was a biography of the American black poet Langston Hughes.

The poetry book, *Revolutionary Petunias & Other Poems,* was nominated for a National Book Award and won the Lillian Smith Award of the Southern Regional Council. The short story collection was titled *In Love and Trouble: Stories of Black Women.* It won a very important prize, the Richard and Hinda Rosenthal Award, given by the American Institute of Arts and Letters.

Alice and her husband moved to New York City in 1974. She accepted a job as contributing editor for the magazine *Ms.* During this period she completed work on her second novel, *Meridian.* She also published her third book of poems.

In 1976 she and her husband were divorced, but they share custody of her daughter, Rebecca Grant. Husband and wife went in different directions.

The amount of her work continued to be amazing. In 1981 she published her second collection of short fiction: *You Can't Keep a Good Woman Down.* The characters in this second collection are more varied than those in the first.

Her greatest achievement was yet to come. In 1982, her third novel, *The Color Purple,* appeared. This is a powerful, often disturbing novel, but the writing cannot be forgotten. Reviewers were enthusiastic. Peter S. Prescott in *Newsweek* called it "an American novel of permanent importance." Reviewers praised its poetic use of language.

The Color Purple was nominated for the National Book Critics Circle award. It won both an American Book Award and the Pulitzer Prize for fiction. It stayed on the *New York Times* list of bestsellers for over 25 weeks. Warner Brothers bought the movie rights for $350,000.

Alice Walker puts her own beliefs and concerns into her writing. Some critics have complained that "the black woman is *always* the most sympathetic character." Alice doesn't disagree. In an interview with Barbara A. Bannon of *Publishers Weekly,* Alice said, "The black woman is one of America's greatest heroes."

She calls herself a *womanist,* a person especially interested in the rights of black women. A black woman is the center of each story in her first collection. Black women play key roles in her other fiction. An article in *Current Biography* talks about "Miss Walker's concern for the lives of black women, especially those who are poor, uneducated, and Southern."

Alice's sympathies arose from her childhood experiences. She was once asked why she writes. She said she wanted to praise "people I love, the people who are thought to be dumb and backward but who were the ones who first taught me to see beauty."

In June 1983 Alice Walker traveled to China with a group of 11 American women writers. This experience made her realize once again that people are alike the world over. Women in China face many of the struggles women in America face. Alice wanted to find a bond with these courageous women.

She gives special praise to a Chinese woman writer, Ding Ling. This remarkable woman has lived through wars and revolutions, persecution and great hardship. She saw loved ones mistreated. One was executed by a firing squad. She was kept in *solitary* imprisonment, all by herself for ten months. Then she was separated from her husband for six years. She was *banished* to Manchuria to raise chickens among the peasants, or farmers. Her only crime was that she tried to write honestly and truthfully about her life.

Through all the hardships, Ding Ling continued to write. For over 50 years she has written story after story, novel after novel. Once she was paraded in disgrace with a dunce's cap on her head. Her spirit was not crushed.

Yet Ding Ling is not bitter. The only thing she regrets is that she lost time. At nearly 80, she said, "Oh, to be 67 again!"

Alice is not a typical tourist. When she came to the Great Wall, China's most famous monument, she was not impressed. She wrote, "I'll never come thousands of miles to see more of man's folly again. What I hate about the Great Wall is the thought of all the workers' bodies buried in it. I hate the *vastness* and *barrenness* of its location. I hate the suffering the women and children attached to the boulders *endured*. I hate its—let's face it, I hate walls."

Alice had an unexpected way of looking at Chinese

clothes. She said, "People are more important than what they wear. Everyone wears basically the same thing: trousers and shirt. And everyone is neat, clean, and *adequately* dressed. No one wears makeup or jewelry. At first, faces look dull. But soon one becomes conscious of the wonderful honesty natural faces *convey*. An honesty more interesting than any ornament."

Alice Walker is a free and original thinker.

UNDERSTANDING WHAT YOU HAVE READ

Finding Another Title

1. Another good title for this selection might be **(a)** Champion of Black Women's Rights **(b)** How the Chinese Differ from Americans **(c)** The American Civil-Rights Movement **(d)** The Pulitzer Prize and How It Is Awarded.

Getting the Main Idea

2. Alice Walker **(a)** is the first person from Georgia to win the Pulitzer Prize **(b)** has written several books of poetry **(c)** is more famous as a poet than as a novelist **(d)** has written from her experience with people and places.

Finding Details

3. Alice was blinded in one eye at the age of **(a)** six **(b)** eight **(c)** 11 **(d)** 14.

4. Alice's first scholarship was to **(a)** Sarah Lawrence College **(b)** the writers' institute in New Hampshire **(c)** Spelman College **(d)** Wellesley College.

5. Muriel Rukeyser was **(a)** a friend of Mr. Walker's **(b)** an editor at a major publisher's **(c)** a poet **(d)** a professor at Jackson State College.

6. *Once* is the title of **(a)** a collection of poems **(b)** a series of essays **(c)** a short-story collection **(d)** a novel.

7. Alice Walker's husband was **(a)** a writer of children's stories **(b)** an editor **(c)** an authority on China **(d)** a civil-rights lawyer.

8. Alice's first novel was titled **(a)** *The Color Purple* **(b)** *The Third Life* **(c)** *Revolutionary Petunias* **(d)** *You Can't Keep a Good Woman Down.*

9. Alice Walker accepted a job as contributing editor to the magazine **(a)** *Poetry* **(b)** *Ms.* **(c)** the *American Scholar* **(d)** *Newsweek.*

10. Alice Walker approved of Chinese **(a)** clothing **(b)** road building **(c)** clever use of cosmetics **(d)** work with jade.

Making Inferences

11. Alice Walker considered her mother to be **(a)** unhappy **(b)** too easily led **(c)** a modern woman **(d)** too quickly discouraged.

12. The BB gun accident **(a)** ruined Alice's life **(b)** caused scar tissue for a lifetime **(c)** caused Alice to hate her brother **(d)** had some good results.

13. Alice had good fortune in college, for she **(a)** had Muriel Rukeyser as a teacher **(b)** wrote her first novel then **(c)** had a collection of short stories published then **(d)** got to know Lisel Mueller.

14. Alice concentrates on the lives of black women because she feels these women **(a)** are often rich and famous **(b)** will interest readers of her books **(c)** have been mistreated and misunderstood **(d)** will send in their life stories for her to write about.

15. Her attitude toward China's Great Wall can be described as **(a)** breathless **(b)** humorous **(c)** approving **(d)** unfavorable.

Predicting What Happens Next

16. After winning the Pulitzer Prize, Alice Walker probably **(a)** wrote only poetry **(b)** continued to describe the lives of black women **(c)** changed her viewpoint of black women **(d)** won the Nobel Peace Prize.

Deciding on the Order of Events

17. The following events are scrambled. Arrange them in proper order, as they happened. Use letters only.
(a) Alice travels to China.
(b) Alice wins the Pulitzer Prize.
(c) Alice's brother accidentally blinds her in one eye.
(d) Alice writes a biography of Langston Hughes.

Inferring Tone

18. The tone of Ding Ling's comment (184), "Oh, to be 67 again!" is meant to be **(a)** light and amusing **(b)** sad and weary **(c)** thoughtful and serious **(d)** angry and bitter.

Separating Facts from Opinions

For each of the following, tell whether the statement is a fact (*F*) or an opinion (*O*).

19. Alice Walker's second novel was better than her first.
20. In China Alice Walker visited the Great Wall.

Understanding Words from Context

21. She was kept in *solitary* imprisonment, all by herself for ten months.
    Solitary (184) means   (a) cruel   (b) easygoing   (c) alone   (d) distant.
22. Then she was separated from her husband for six years. She was *banished* to Manchuria to raise chickens among the peasants, or farmers.
    Banished (184) means   (a) sent away   (b) called back   (c) flown   (d) written.
23. Alice is concerned with the suffering that people lived through. She wrote, "I hate the suffering the women and children attached to the boulders *endured.*"
    Endured (184) means   (a) read about   (b) spoke about   (c) wrote about   (d) experienced.
24. Alice commented on the fact that everyone had enough clothes. She wrote: "Everyone is neat, clean, and *adequately* dressed."
    Adequately (185) means   (a) poorly   (b) well enough   (c) showily   (d) strangely.
25. "But soon one becomes conscious of the wonderful honesty natural faces *convey*. An honesty more interesting than any ornament."
    Convey (185) means   (a) conceal   (b) suggest   (c) poke fun at   (d) imitate.

THINKING IT OVER

1. How did Alice Walker's childhood affect her writing later?
2. What disadvantages did Alice have? How did she rise above them?
3. How did Alice show that she is an original thinker?
4. Some writers become successful as novelists; some become successful as poets. How did Alice show she could write in many different literary forms?
5. Most tourists who stand at the Great Wall of China are impressed by its great size. What was Alice Walker's reaction? Why did she react this way?
6. Alice Walker seems to think that wearing simple clothes and wearing no cosmetics would be a good idea. Do you agree? Why do people wear expensive clothes? Why do they use cosmetics?
7. Alice is a strong feminist. She thinks many women are still at a disadvantage in the United States. Do you agree? Explain.
8. Is a childhood on the farm better than a childhood in the city? What do you think?

ANOTHER LOOK AT THE QUOTATION

Those who try to do something and fail are infinitely better than those who try to do nothing and succeed.

RICHARD BIRD

1. Explain the quotation in your own words.
2. What is Richard Bird's attitude toward people who don't try? How can someone succeed at doing nothing?

3. How do you feel if you fail at something? Is it possible to learn from failure? How?

4. Should we be content with failure? What should be our attitude toward a failing test, for example?

WORDS AT YOUR SERVICE—SUFFIXES

> *"What I hate about the Great Wall is the thought of all the workers' bodies buried in it. I hate the* vastness *and* barrenness *of its location." (184)*

Notice those two words, *vastness* and *barrenness*. They have something in common: the suffix *ness*. Suffixes, the third of our word parts, can often be helpful. The suffix *ness* means *state of, condition of.* Thus *vastness* is the *state of being vast, huge. Barrenness* is the state of being *barren, empty.* The Great Wall is located in a great empty location.

The suffix *ness* appears in many other words:

carelessness—state of being careless

emptiness—state of being empty

happiness—state of being happy

openness—state of being open

stubbornness—state of being stubborn

How many more can you add?

Here are some other helpful suffixes:

Suffix	Meaning	Example	Definition of the Example Word
an, ian	one who	music*ian*	*one who* plays music
en	make	hard*en*	*make* hard
ish	like, related to	child*ish*	*like* a child

ist	one who	dent*ist*	*one who* works on teeth
ship	state of, quality of	partner*ship*	*state of* being a partner

Fill in the blank in each sentence below by supplying the missing suffix from the list above. The number in parentheses tells you how many letters you need.

EXAMPLE

The state of sad_____ seems almost natural for some people. (4)

Insert the suffix *ness*. The complete word is *sadness*.

1. One who works with magic is a magic_____. (3)
2. A person who acts like a fool is fool_____. (3)
3. The state of being an owner is owner_____. (4)
4. Make that dress a little shorter; short_____ it. (2)
5. One who rides a bicycle is a cycl_____. (3)

COMPLETING AN OUTLINE

The article on Alice Walker might be outlined in the following way. Five outline items have been omitted. Test your understanding of the structure of the article by following the directions after the outline.

I. Early years
   A. Birth in Eatonton, Georgia
   B. Alice, the young writer
   C. Shooting accident
   D.
   E. Scholarship to Spelman College

II. Interest in civil rights
   A. Transfer to Sarah Lawrence College
   B. Travel to Africa
   C. Writing fellowship
   D.
   E. Move to Mississippi

III. Literary success
   A. Publication of book of poetry
   B. First novel
   C. Other early publications
   D.
   E. Many other awards

IV. Alice Walker's message
   A. Alice, the *womanist*
   B.
   C. Tribute to the people of her youth

V. Her trip to China
   A. Her concern for Chinese women
   B.
   C. Approval of Chinese ways

Fill in the items omitted from the outline. Correctly match the items in column A with the outline numbers in column B.

A	B
1. The Pulitzer Prize	a. I. D.
2. Tribute to Ding Ling	b. II. D.
3. Success in high school	c. III. D.
4. Marriage to a civil-rights lawyer	d. IV. B.
5. Concern for black women	e. V. B.

ANOTHER LOOK

HOW MUCH DO YOU REMEMBER?

1. The person who wanted to write novels about knights is **(a)** Sir Arthur Conan Doyle **(b)** Agatha Christie **(c)** Alice Walker **(d)** Max Mallowan.
2. The creator of Miss Marple is **(a)** Sir Arthur Conan Doyle **(b)** Edgar Allan Poe **(c)** Archibald Christie **(d)** Agatha Christie.
3. The person who was born in Haiti is **(a)** Sir Arthur Conan Doyle **(b)** Sir Walter Scott **(c)** John James Audubon **(d)** Jack Hawkins.
4. The person who lost the sight of one eye in an accident is **(a)** Edgar Allan Poe **(b)** Alice Walker **(c)** John James Audubon **(d)** Agatha Christie.
5. The person whose wife played a key role in his success is **(a)** Sir Arthur Conan Doyle **(b)** John James Audubon **(c)** Robert Havell **(d)** Hercule Poirot.
6. The person who won a Pulitzer Prize is **(a)** Edgar Allan Poe **(b)** Ding Ling **(c)** Alexander Wilson **(d)** Alice Walker.
7. A bird that is extinct, or gone from the earth, is the **(a)** phoebe **(b)** blue-gray gnatcatcher **(c)** passenger pigeon **(d)** black-throated blue warbler.
8. The person who has been pictured on U.S. postage stamps is **(a)** John James Audubon **(b)** Alice Walker **(c)** Muriel Rukeyser **(d)** Melvyn Leventhal.

9. A fictional character that many think of as a real person is (a) Miss Marple (b) Sherlock Holmes (c) Dr. Joseph Bell (d) Micah Clarke.
10. There is still an unsolved mystery in the life of (a) Sir Arthur Conan Doyle (b) Lucy Audubon (c) Sir Walter Scott (d) Agatha Christie.

WHAT IS YOUR OPINION?

1. Audubon was more successful in Europe than in the United States. Why are people sometimes more successful in countries other than their own?
2. Which of the four subjects made the most important contribution to humanity? Defend your choice.
3. What causes boredom? What do you do when you are bored?
4. Why do you suppose Doyle got bored with Sherlock Holmes and Agatha Christie with Hercule Poirot?
5. How did selfishness and greed bring on the end of the passenger pigeon?

THE QUOTATION AND THE UNIT

We can do anything we want to do if we stick to it long enough.

HELEN KELLER

1. Explain the quotation in your own words.
2. Do you agree with the quotation? Are there limits to what we can do? Explain.
3. Helen Keller, as you probably know, was blind and deaf. Yet she led a full and productive life. Do you think she followed her own advice? Explain.
4. Did the subjects in this chapter stick to what they wanted to do? In what ways?

SHAPERS OF THE MODERN WORLD

The higher you climb on the mountain, the harder the wind blows.

SAM CUMMINGS

People shape events. Who knows what the world would have been like without great leaders like George Washington, or evil leaders like Adolf Hitler? Throughout history, outstanding men and women have changed the course of human events.

The three subjects in Unit 4 have all helped to shape history in their own way. Two of the subjects are political leaders. The third, I. M. Pei, by his brilliant architecture, has helped to shape the way we live and work. He is a shaper in a physical sense. But his life also shows that members of minority groups in America can reach the top.

Jomo Kenyatta was a giant among the leaders of Africa. He

played a major role in the birth of Kenya as a free nation. By his own greatness of spirit, he showed that cruelty, violence, and revenge have no place in government.

Luis Muñoz Marin played an important role in Puerto Rico. As its leader, he brought the island through many difficult and discouraging times. He, too, kept his hope alive and acted as an inspiration for his fellow Puerto Ricans.

All three subjects showed wisdom, good judgment, faith in their jobs, and willingness to take the bad with the good. These people truly helped shape the world of today.

I. M. PEI:
Master Architect

We shape our buildings; thereafter they shape us.

WINSTON CHURCHILL

The next time you leave your home, look at each building you pass. What general feeling do you get? Select one specific building. Is it refreshing to look at? Does it have a pleasing shape? Does it seem to belong where it is?

Look at the details of the building. Notice any special features. Are the windows well placed? Are there columns, or large posts, in front of the building? What ornaments are included? Is the roof sloping? Is it flat? Are there arches, domes, or steeples?

Like people, buildings and other structures have personalities of their own. Some buildings are world-famous. For example, everyone recognizes a picture of the Leaning Tower of Pisa and connects it with Italy. The Eiffel Tower immediately identifies Paris. The Pyramids and the Sphinx are associated with Egypt.

All these structures were designed by architects. Because he gave his name to the structure itself, we know the name of the architect who created the Eiffel Tower. No one, however, knows the names of the ancient architects who planned the temples of Greece or the Colosseum in Rome.

Architects dream in stone, wood, and other *structural* materials. A writer uses words to bring dreams to reality. A painter uses oils, watercolors, or some other substances. A composer of music combines notes to make a song or a symphony. Architects do not deal in these delicate substances. Architects must work with wood, stone, metal, concrete, and many new substances. An architect is both an artist and a scientist.

Each period in history is famous for certain kinds of architecture. The ancient world produced the Egyptian pyramids and the temples of Greece and Rome. In the Middle Ages, great cathedrals showed the influence of the religious spirit of the time. Great palaces and luxurious private residences characterize the later Middle Ages. In modern times the skyscraper suggests business and wealth.

The history of American architecture can be studied by looking at buildings still standing. Scattered throughout the country are buildings of the Colonial period, built before the American Revolution. Some are in specially preserved places like Sturbridge, Massachusetts, or Williamsburg, Virginia. Others are tucked away between more modern buildings in eastern cities like Boston, New York, Philadelphia, and Charleston, South Carolina. Perhaps some Colonial buildings still stand in your neighborhood.

There was a Federal style, just after the Revolution. Federal buildings were often made of brick. They had simple lines, but they pleased the eye. Many buildings of this period still exist. The Harris House, in Castleton, Vermont, for example, was built about 1800. It is still a beautiful building.

The next style is called Greek Revival. *Revival* means *rebirth*. Houses imitated Greek temples. This style was popular from about 1820 to 1860. It is the style of the beautiful southern plantation houses. *Tara,* Scarlett O'Hara's home in *Gone With the Wind,* is in this style. These houses often had columns, large white posts, in front. You will find many imitations of this style around the country. Today even small houses on crowded streets sometimes have columns in front. This design often looks out of place on city streets, but it probably seems grand to the people who live in these houses.

Many other styles can be traced from the Victorian period, beginning about 1840. In fact, several styles may exist, at one time. Even today some architects design buildings in the style of an earlier time.

There are many great names in modern architecture.

Designers like Louis Sullivan and Philip Johnson helped give us the modern skyscraper. Edward Durrell Stone created many beautiful buildings, including the United States embassy in New Delhi, India. Frank Lloyd Wright built many private homes of unusual beauty.

One of the most interesting of all modern architects is the Chinese American Ieoh Ming Pei.* He is also one of the busiest. His designs beautify cities around the world, from Singapore to Boston.

Pei was born in Canton, China, in 1917. He was the son of one of China's leading bankers. The family moved to Shanghai, where he spent most of his childhood. In 1935, Pei left China for the United States. He took a program combining architecture and engineering at the Massachusetts Institute of Technology.

As he looks back on this move, he says, "It was my good fortune I went to Boston to study. Boston has a long tradition in the China trade, and my father had many friends there. So I was able to enter Boston society very early on, long before I managed to speak English. So I really had a rather comfortable experience as a foreign student in this country."

In college, Pei met his wife, Eileen Loo. She was a student at nearby Wellesley College. They were married in 1942. Pei fully intended to return to China after getting his bachelor of architecture degree. But the outbreak of World War II changed his plans.

He and his wife moved to Princeton, New Jersey. He served on the National Defense Research Committee. This committee developed information on Japanese architecture for the war effort.

When World War II ended, revolution broke out in

---

* Pronounced PAY.

China. Again, Pei could not return. Instead he taught at the graduate school of design at Harvard University.

At this time the Harvard school was very much concerned with modern architecture. Two great European architects, Marcel Breuer and Walter Gropius, influenced Harvard students. They provided a new approach to architecture. Pei became a part of this modern movement.

As the writer Peter Lemos said, modern architecture "was not simply a new way of designing buildings." Its aim was to provide low-cost buildings with simple but beautiful shapes. Pei was given a chance to try out his new ideas. In 1948 the real estate executive William Zeckendorf hired him as a designer. Pei worked for Zeckendorf for 12 years.

During this period Pei designed many famous buildings, including the Mile High Center in Denver and the Place Ville Marie in Montreal. His work helped change government standards for apartment projects.

In 1955 Pei began doing work on his own. By 1960 he had established his own firm. Many of the architects who joined him then are still with him. Such long associations are rare in architecture.

Pei gives his architects plenty of responsibility. He says, "If you want to do a lot of work, and to do it well, then you have to learn to *delegate* [in order] to use your own time to the greatest benefit. I like to think that is exactly what I have been doing."

After he had set up his own firm, Pei designed many buildings for his former college, the Massachusetts Institute of Technology. He did other work in Boston. He designed a new West Wing for the Boston Museum of Fine Arts. Perhaps his most important project was to design the John F. Kennedy Library.

Pei was a little-known architect when President Kennedy's widow, Jacqueline, invited him to design the library. The Kennedy family's confidence was justified. When the library was opened in 1979, the building was widely admired.

Life rarely runs smoothly all the time. Pei had an unhappy experience with another Boston building. He completed the John Hancock Tower in the early 1970s. This 70-story building is a beautiful structure. It has so many windows that the sides seem almost to float in reflections from the sky and from other buildings.

Then, unexpectedly, windows started popping out and crashing to the street below. Pei and his firm had to *put up with* a lot of criticism even though they were not to blame. Courts have since ruled that the manufacturer of the glass was at fault. But for a while, until the problem was solved, Pei's firm had lean times. Government work is not enough. As Pei said of the disaster: "During the early '70s, it almost cut off all *corporate* work from our practice, and that's a very, very serious loss; but we survived."

Now the windows are securely fastened. The tower is considered one of the firm's greatest successes. It is becoming an important landmark for Boston. Pei's firm has prospered, and his assignments are many.

A list of Pei's buildings is a roll call of modern architecture. The East Building of the National Gallery of Art in Washington, D.C., is one of his finest efforts. Visitors from around the world make this a *must* stop.

When Pei had a *setback* because of those falling windows he didn't let it defeat him. He went abroad. He looked for overseas clients—and got them. He completed important projects in Kuwait, Singapore, and Hong Kong. He visited China in 1974 for the first time in 40 years and began advising the government on building projects. In 1979 he was asked to design the Fragrant Hill Hotel there.

Pei still feels close to China. When he won the $100,000 Pritzker Prize, he used the money for Chinese students. He has one rule. After they graduate, the students must return to China.

The Louvre, in Paris, is one of the world's great museums. By the 1980s it had outgrown its space, and the French government wanted to make it larger. The government asked Pei to design the expansion. After six months' study, he accepted the assignment. His plans for the new areas have aroused discussion and disagreement, but no one can deny that his ideas are brilliant.

I. M. Pei is an interesting person. He is so busy that he says, "It sounds as if I haven't managed my life very well. Success came to me very late, and I have to do it now. Where someone else might be able to enjoy life as they grow older, I can't." Then he smiles as if to say, "What's the difference? I'm having a wonderful time!"

He lives surrounded by art. His town house in New York is filled with paintings by modern artists. His office contains art objects fit for a museum. His taste in art reflects his taste in architecture.

On the subject of modern architecture, he has some things to say: "Today architecture is going in ten different directions. You have to jump up and down, stand on your head, and do all sorts of things. I don't do that; therefore I am not interesting to the critics. I don't do something new every five days, so I have been called a *conservative*. I like that. . . . When you do something that lasts a long time, you can't just close your eyes and say, 'I'm on to new things now, don't look at that anymore.' I don't think that that's what architecture should be."

Pei's beautiful architecture shows the influence of that point of view. He is truly a shaper of the modern world.

UNDERSTANDING WHAT YOU HAVE READ

Finding Another Title

1. Another good title for this selection might be **(a)** Modern Architecture and I. M. Pei **(b)** How to Succeed as an Architect **(c)** The Periods of American Architecture **(d)** I. M. Pei's Work Abroad.

Getting the Main Idea

2. I. M. Pei **(a)** created the John F. Kennedy Library **(b)** once had a bad experience with a building in Boston **(c)** used his experience to become an excellent architect **(d)** once worked for another firm, but now has his own.

Finding Details

3. The famous Leaning Tower is in **(a)** France **(b)** Egypt **(c)** Greece **(d)** Italy.
4. Two states mentioned that have specially preserved buildings are **(a)** New York and Pennsylvania **(b)** Virginia and Massachusetts **(c)** South Carolina and Virginia **(d)** Massachusetts and South Carolina.
5. The large white posts, or columns, in front of a house may mean that the house was built in the **(a)** Federal style **(b)** Greek Revival style **(c)** Colonial period **(d)** Victorian period.
6. The United States embassy in New Delhi, India, was designed by **(a)** Frank Lloyd Wright **(b)** Louis Sullivan **(c)** I. M. Pei **(d)** Edward Durrell Stone.

7. Pei could not go back to China after college because
   (a) war had broken out   (b) his wife had just had
   a child   (c) he had no money   (d) China had no
   need for architects.
8. Pei got his first teaching job at   (a) Wellesley College   (b) the Massachusetts Institute of Technology   (c) Harvard University   (d) Princeton University.
9. The difficulty with the John Hancock Tower was
   with its   (a) size   (b) structure   (c) windows   (d)
   roof.
10. All the following places are mentioned as having
    Pei buildings EXCEPT   (a) Kuwait   (b) Japan
    (c) Singapore   (d) Hong Kong.

Making Inferences

11. All buildings   (a) tell something about their de-
    signers   (b) show the influence of I. M. Pei   (c)
    should be made of wood or stone   (d) are in Colo-
    nial style or modern style.
12. The mansion *Tara* in *Gone With the Wind* had   (a)
    porches on three sides   (b) columns in front   (c)
    red-brick fireplaces in every room   (d) an attached
    barn for the animals.
13. Pei's family in China was   (a) unhappy   (b) huge
    (c) poor   (d) wealthy.
14. Pei's architects are loyal to him because   (a) they
    have no other job opportunities   (b) he sends them
    on trips for their vacations   (c) he treats them well
    (d) they wouldn't live anywhere else but New York.
15. The bad luck with the John Hancock Tower may
    have been good luck because   (a) Pei had to go
    abroad to get new customers   (b) he met Jacque-

line Kennedy at that time (c) it gave Pei a long rest (d) he got a lot of publicity, even if it was bad.

Predicting What Happens Next

16. I. M. Pei will probably (a) retire at 65 (b) cut his staff of architects in half (c) refuse to build another hotel in China (d) continue to accept overseas projects.

Deciding on the Order of Events

17. The following events are scrambled. Arrange them in proper order, as they happened. Use letters only.
    (a) Pei attends the Massachusetts Institute of Technology.
    (b) The John F. Kennedy Library opens.
    (c) Eileen Loo and Pei are married.
    (d) Pei establishes his own firm of architects.

Inferring Tone

18. When Pei says he hasn't managed his life well (203), he is really (a) angry (b) joking (c) sad (d) serious.

Separating Facts from Opinions

For each of the following, tell whether the statement is a fact (*F*) or an opinion (*O*).
19. Pei builds better skyscrapers than did earlier architects like Louis Sullivan.
20. Many examples of the Greek Revival style exist throughout the country.

Understanding Words from Context

21. Architects dream in stone, wood, and other *structural* materials.
    Structural means (a) lightweight (b) colorful (c) pleasing to the touch (d) used in building.
22. Pei gives his architects plenty of responsibility. He says, "If you want to do a lot of work, and to do it well, then you have to learn to *delegate* [in order] to use your own time to the greatest benefit."
    Delegate means (a) assign a job to someone else (b) keep going over plans (c) find a new way to do something (d) never admit defeat.
23. Government work is not enough. As Pei said of the disaster: "During the early '70s, it almost cut off all *corporate* work from our practice, and that's a very, very serious loss; but we survived."
    Corporate means (a) legal (b) financially profitable (c) dealing with skyscrapers (d) provided by businesses.
24. When Pei had a *setback* because of those falling windows, he didn't let it defeat him. He went abroad.
    Setback means (a) bad publicity (b) reverse in fortune (c) argument (d) disappointment.
25. "I don't do something new every five days, so I have been called a *conservative*."
    Conservative means a person who (a) enjoys change for change's sake (b) wants to preserve older values (c) dislikes most architecture (d) would rather read a book than watch television.

THINKING IT OVER

1. If the purpose of a building is to provide shelter, why worry about what it looks like? Do you think that a building may have another use too? If so, what is it?
2. Have you followed the suggestions at the beginning of this chapter? Have you noticed the buildings in your own neighborhood? What have you discovered that you never noticed before?
3. Why are skyscrapers built in downtown city areas and usually not out in the country? Why are small private houses rarely built in downtown areas?
4. How did Pei show his intelligence and courage after the problem with the John Hancock Tower in Boston?
5. Why do modern architects build skyscrapers in reinforced concrete? Why not use just stone, as the builders of cathedrals did?
6. How did Jacqueline Kennedy help Pei's career?
7. Pei has more than enough money to live on. Why does he continue to have such a busy schedule, with little time for relaxation?
8. In a humorous mood, Frank Lloyd Wright once said, "A doctor can bury his mistakes, but an architect can only advise his clients to plant vines." What is the serious point behind this lighthearted comment?

ANOTHER LOOK AT THE QUOTATION

We shape our buildings; thereafter they shape us.

WINSTON CHURCHILL

1. Explain the quotation in your own words.
2. How are people affected, or shaped, by the buildings they live in? Think about buildings you are in regularly. How are you influenced by the house you live in? By the school you go to? By the church or temple you attend?
3. Why were ancient Greek temples built in stone? How do changes in available material affect the houses that are built? Of what materials do you think houses of the future will be built?

WORDS AT YOUR SERVICE—IDIOMS

> *Pei and his firm had to* put up with *a lot of criticism even though they were not to blame. Courts have since ruled that the manufacturer of the glass was at fault. (202)*

No doubt you understand what the phrase *put up with* means. However, if you try to get the meaning of the phrase by looking at the individual words, you would have difficulty. By themselves, *put, up,* and *with* have nothing to do with *accept.* Together they mean something like *accept, take:*

> *Pei and his firm had to* take *a lot of criticism.*

Notice that *put up with* seems a better choice than *take.*

Put up with is an example of something that exists in every language. It is called an *idiom.* An idiom is an expression that cannot be translated word for word into another language. The total meaning of the words in an idiom is different from the meanings of the individual words.

A highway near LaGuardia Airport in New York had a grass border. On the border was a sign that read: "Give the grass a break." Foreigners who saw the sign wondered why motorists were told to injure the grass. The opposite is true. "Give the grass a break" means "Don't injure the grass." *To give a break* is to *do a favor* for someone. This is another example of an idiom.

English is filled with idioms. Can you tell what each of the following means? Study the sentences below and then guess at the meaning of each *italicized* idiom. Remember that an idiom doesn't mean what the individual words seem to mean.

EXAMPLE

Martina *made no bones* about her desire to win her sixth Wimbledon title.
Made no bones means (a) was doubtful (b) made clear (c) talked nervously (d) repeated over and over again.
The idiom *made no bones* is an expression of confidence. The correct answer is (b) *made clear.*

1. Van wanted Gerald to invest in a get-rich-quick scheme, but Gerald told him to *go fly a kite.*
   Go fly a kite means (a) start a new hobby (b) speak more clearly (c) experiment with electricity (d) go away.

2. Whenever Jennie doesn't get enough sleep, she is *out of sorts.*
   Out of sorts means (a) out of doors (b) unlucky (c) irritable (d) comical.

3. I like to practice my violin *every now and then.*
   Every now and then means (a) occasionally (b) often (c) all the time (d) never.
4. Don't keep asking. I'll get to cutting the lawn *right away.*
   Right away means (a) skillfully (b) immediately (c) cheerfully (d) properly.
5. Shy Ted finally got up enough nerve to *pop the question* to Sheila.
   Pop the question means (a) ask to dinner (b) ask about a date (c) propose (d) marry.

COMPLETING AN OUTLINE

The article on I. M. Pei might be outlined in the following way. Five outline items have been omitted. Test your understanding of the structure of the article by following the directions after the outline.

I. Buildings and architects
   A.
   B. Famous buildings of the past
   C. The architect's materials
   D. American architecture

II. Early years of I. M. Pei
   A. Birth in China
   B.
   C. Marriage
   D. Work for the war effort

III. First successes as an architect
   A. Teaching at Harvard
   B.
   C. Famous buildings

IV. Pei and his own firm
    A. The John F. Kennedy Library
    B.
    C. International projects

V. Pei the man
    A. Busy life
    B. Taste in art
    C.

Fill in the items omitted from the outline. Correctly match the items in column A with the outline numbers in column B.

A	B
1. Trouble with the John Hancock Tower	a. I. A.
2. Study in the U.S.	b. II. B.
3. Thoughts on architecture	c. III. B.
4. The personality of buildings	d. IV. B.
5. Work for Zeckendorf	e. V. C.

JOMO KENYATTA:
The Lion of Kenya

His heart was as great as the world, but there was no room in it to hold the memory of a wrong.

RALPH WALDO EMERSON

Most Americans know very little about Africa. Some people think of it as a vast, dense jungle, with lions and tigers roaming around. Actually, the lion prefers the plains, where game is more plentiful. And the tiger is not a native African animal at all. These errors are typical of wrong ideas about Africa.

There are three basic things you should know about Africa: it is huge; it has great variety; and it has a fascinating history.

As a continent, Africa is second only to Asia in size. It is three times larger than the United States (including Alaska and Hawaii). It stretches 5,000 miles from Cape Town in the south to Tunis in the north. The distance from New York City to San Francisco is only half that amount.

Africa is a continent that shows variety in all things. This large land area contains deserts and grasslands, plains and mountains, cool highlands and steamy jungles. You can leave the tropical heat of the jungle in Kenya and climb to the frozen top of Kilimanjaro. The people, too, are varied. The tiny Bushmen in the south are very different from the tall Watusi in East Africa.

The history of Africa is not well known. Paintings on Sahara rocks go back 8,000 years. These paintings give us some clues. They show that the Sahara Desert was then a fertile region with rivers and grassy valleys. The rock paintings trace history for us. They tell of newcomers on the scene and of times of plenty. They record change and growth. They show art, music, and dancing.

About 4,000 years ago the Sahara began to dry up. The people living in the Sahara had to learn new ways of living. They could no longer raise cattle, because cattle could not survive in the dry regions. Then invading hunters drove away the peaceful cattle herders. The camel replaced the horse as a beast of burden.

A similar story happened in other African areas, with hunters and cattle herders in *conflict*. But there were long periods of peace, too. Some areas became stable. Civilizations grew. Empires were born.

In the fourteenth century the kingdom of Mali became rich and powerful. It had swallowed up the ancient kingdom of Ghana, but then it was threatened in turn. The Songhai Empire gradually took over Mali and extended its power eastward. Still further eastward, the Kanem-Bornu Empire grew strong. It lasted a thousand years. Some travelers from Europe visited these old kingdoms and reported their experiences when they returned.

After a while European nations became interested in Africa. The French, Italians, British, Portuguese, Spanish, Belgians, and Dutch came to trade. Some stayed on and absorbed African tribes and kingdoms into their own empires. Until the end of World War II, Africa had few independent nations.

World War II changed all that. The winds of freedom began to blow across the face of Africa. In 1957, Ghana became the first African country to become free under its outspoken president, Kwame Nkrumah. Other nations soon followed. In 1960 alone, 17 former African colonies gained their independence peacefully. Harold Macmillan, prime minister of Britain, said, "It is happening everywhere. The wind of change is blowing through the continent and, whether we like it or not, the growth of national consciousness is a political fact. We must all accept it."

The names of the new African nations often recall their past glories: Benin, Botswana, Burundi, Rwanda, Tanzania, Zambia. These were the names of proud peoples, powerful kingdoms, successful civilizations. Of all the new African nations, one of the most important is Kenya.

Like most other nations, Kenya has had a stormy history. In the 1950s, Kenya was torn by some very bitter fighting. Yet a generation later Kenya was considered one of the most *stable* of the new nations. Credit for many of Kenya's solid achievements must go to Jomo Kenyatta, who first became premier and then president of the new country.

Jomo Kenyatta himself had a long and productive life. He lived through difficulties that would have broken an ordinary person. But he kept his head. He sought the good of his country. His personality helped to keep the many different Kenyan tribes at peace with each other.

Besides the different tribal societies, Kenya is also the home of many European settlers and Asiatic shopkeepers. Kenyatta tried to keep peace among various groups. When seeking independence from England, he said, "We do not think in tribal terms. Our aim is not to select a man because he is black or brown, but on his *capability.* We have no room for dictatorship in Kenya. We believe in democratic government." Jomo Kenyatta largely succeeded in making Kenya democratic.

Kenyatta disliked *pettiness* and a mean spirit. He lived a long life and suffered much, but he was forgiving. He realized that people need education, guidance, and opportunity to grow.

Jomo Kenyatta got his name from the *kinyata,* an embroidered belt he liked to wear. His original name was Kamau Ngengi. He was born in a Kikuyu tribal region near Mount Kenya. As a child, he tended his father's herds. Each animal looked different. He had to know every animal in the herd by its *distinctive* markings. Once he was tested. His father's animals were mixed with many other animals. He successfully picked out the right animals. Later his keen powers of observation would again help him.

The young boy was not satisfied with being a herder, though. He wanted an education. For a while he attended a mission school, but again he was dissatisfied. He ran away to Nairobi, the main city of Kenya. There he became a leader of the young Africans and acquired the name *Kenyatta.* He began to organize schools for Kikuyu children.

In 1928, Kenyatta became secretary of a group that sought independence for Africa. Kenyatta dreamed even wilder dreams. He wanted someday to unite Kenya into an independent nation. In *Leaders of New Nations,* Leonard Kenworthy and Emma Ferrari point out, "How could one unite and develop a country whose people were divided into various closely knit tribes; whose land, with almost no natural resources, was three-fifths unproductive desert?" Besides, "ways of earning a living were limited to the most primitive forms of agriculture, with few crops that could be sold for money." The people were victims of poverty, ignorance, and disease.

Kenyatta started a Kikuyu newspaper, but he was impatient with the slow progress toward his goal. He visited London and made many friends. He also visited Moscow, and Berlin and Hamburg in Germany. After 18 months, he returned to Kenya a famous man. Prime ministers and presidents saw in him a leader of the new Africa, the Africa to come.

Because the British controlled Kenya, Kenyatta decided that progress toward independence would have to be made in London. He went back and stayed there 15 years, all that time struggling to win freedom for his land. He sent requests to the British government. He wrote letters to newspapers. He spoke to large audiences. He helped organize the Pan-African Federation. During this period he even appeared in a movie with Paul Robeson, the great American singer.

Kenyatta continued his own education. He studied English. He enrolled at the London School of Economics. An expert on African tribal life, he was often in demand as a speaker. At this time he also wrote a book, *Facing Mount Kenya*. This was an excellent study of African tribal society.

During World War II, Kenyatta worked as a laborer in England. After the war he was restless to return home. Just before leaving for Kenya, he wrote a pamphlet. In "Kenya, Land of Conflict," he warned that revolution might break out if independence were not granted. He was right.

In Kenya again, Kenyatta became president of the African National Union. By 1951 it had 150,000 members. The British resisted all efforts at independence, and the settlers became uneasy. Then a kind of civil war broke out.

The Mau Mau was a secret society that preached violence against the white settlers. Both sides performed cruel acts. The British accused Kenyatta of being the secret leader of the Mau Mau. Kenyatta denied this charge. He said he preferred peaceful methods, not violence.

The British did not believe Kenyatta. He was arrested on October 20, 1952. He was brought to trial and convicted. In his last speech at the trial, Kenyatta said these famous words: "We look forward to the day when peace shall come to this land and when the truth shall be known that we, as African leaders, have stood for peace. We stand for the rights of the African people, that Africa may find a place among the nations." Once again he cried out against violence.

Kenyatta was put in prison, and the struggle got worse. His imprisonment united most Kenyans against British rule. Gradually, the British gave more and more rights to the Kenyans. Kenyatta's followers called for his release with the cry, *"Uhuru na Kenyatta"* (Freedom and Kenyatta).

When Kenyatta was released, he got a hero's welcome. This remarkable man refused to think of revenge. "The past is dead," he said. "It is the future that is living."

Step by step, Kenya moved toward independence. Finally, on December 12, 1963, Kenya became independent. Kenyatta became premier and then president. He had reached a goal that once had seemed impossible.

Independence didn't solve all Kenya's problems. There were all kinds of difficulties. The old problems remained, and new ones sprang up. Kenyatta needed foreign aid, but he didn't want foreign influence or control. He wanted Kenya to be strong as well as free. He said, "Now that we have *Uhuru,* the next thing is to build the nation. Now I must see the progress, see the standard of living raised."

Kenyatta's policies were challenged inside the country. New people rose to seek positions of leadership. In May 1966 a major election was held. Kenyatta was then in his late seventies.

As Jules Archer says, in *African Firebrand,* "The lion of Kenya waited tensely for the results of the election to tell him whether he still had the confidence of his people, or whether his life's work was over. When the returns were counted, they showed a landslide victory for Jomo Kenyatta."

The years that followed were not easy. New problems sprang up. New threats appeared. The neighboring nation of Uganda was thrown into confusion by the rise of General Idi Amin to almost unlimited power. His own country's problems continued to bother Kenyatta. But he never lost his sense of balance.

Throughout his years of power, Kenyatta stayed close

to the soil. He lived simply in a farmhouse in the area of his birth. He could look out toward Mount Kenya, the inspiration of his life.

Like all leaders in public life, Kenyatta had his enemies. Not everyone agreed with him. But all agreed he was something special. He had grown from a young herder to become a skillful leader. He protected his people, black and white. The *Lion of Kenya,* as he was called, had earned respect.

Kenyatta could truly be called the "father of his country." When he died on August 22, 1978, the whole world mourned.

There is a Swahili expression used by tree loggers: *"Harambee."* It means "Let's all pull together." *"Harambee"* has become the battle cry of Kenyatta's Kenya. *"Harambee!"* Perhaps the rest of the world could use that expression, too.

UNDERSTANDING WHAT YOU HAVE READ

Finding Another Title

1. Another good title for this selection might be **(a)** A History of Ghana **(b)** Freedom and Cooperation **(c)** A Wise and Forgiving Leader of His People **(d)** New African Nations.

Getting the Main Idea

2. Jomo Kenyatta seemed to be very **(a)** small in size **(b)** wise **(c)** violent **(d)** afraid to become a leader.

Finding Details

3. The first African records go back (a) 6,000 years (b) 8,000 years (c) to 2000 B.C. (d) to when the Sahara began to dry up.
4. The kingdom of Ghana was taken over by the kingdom of (a) Kanem-Bornu (b) Kenya (c) Uganda (d) Mali.
5. All the following European nations are mentioned as coming to Africa EXCEPT the (a) Belgians (b) Norwegians (c) Dutch (d) French.
6. Tanzania is mentioned as (a) the birthplace of Jomo Kenyatta (b) another name for Mali (c) a source of high-grade uranium (d) a new African nation.
7. Kenyatta got his name from (a) the country Kenya (b) a belt he wore (c) his father's family (d) an English friend.
8. *Facing Mount Kenya* is a book about (a) mountains (b) snakes and lizards (c) African tribes (d) independence for Kenya.
9. "Kenya, Land of Conflict" was written by (a) an English leader (b) two Americans (c) Jomo Kenyatta (d) the president of Botswana.
10. *Harambee* means (a) Let's work together (b) The past is dead (c) Freedom! (d) Progress!

Making Inferences

11. The distance from New York City to San Francisco is mentioned to (a) show how large the United States is (b) compare the United States with Ghana (c) show how much more efficient air travel is than surface travel (d) show how large Africa is.

12. During his stay in England, Kenyatta probably learned a great deal about **(a)** tribal life in his own country **(b)** tank warfare **(c)** the Europeans' way of looking at things **(d)** growing fruits and vegetables.
13. Any connection between Kenyatta and the Mau Mau **(a)** was never proved **(b)** was not believed by the British government **(c)** was proved beyond all doubt at the trial **(d)** was never mentioned in Kenya.
14. *Swahili* is the name of **(a)** a language **(b)** an animal **(c)** a man **(d)** a place.
15. The last sentence of the selection (page 220) suggests that the world needs **(a)** more arms and planes **(b)** cooperation **(c)** a single world leader **(d)** kindness to animals.

Predicting What Happens Next

16. When he came to power, Kenyatta probably **(a)** threw all the white settlers out of the country **(b)** tried to get the whites and the blacks to work together **(c)** took a year's vacation in London **(d)** put everyone who disagreed with him in jail.

Deciding on the Order of Events

17. The following events are scrambled. Arrange them in proper order, as they happened.
    (a) Kenyatta is jailed by the British.
    (b) Kenyatta becomes president of Kenya.
    (c) Kenyatta visits London for the first time.
    (d) Kenyatta gets his name from a belt he wore.

Inferring Tone

18. The tone of Harold Macmillan's statement about Africa (215) is **(a)** happy **(b)** doubtful **(c)** serious **(d)** cruel.

Separating Facts from Opinions

For each of the following, tell whether the statement is a fact (*F*) or an opinion (*O*).

19. Jomo Kenyatta was the first president of Kenya.
20. The British were justified in jailing Kenyatta when they did.

Understanding Words from Context

21. A similar story happened in other African areas, with hunters and cattle herders in *conflict*. But there were long periods of peace, too.
Conflict (215) means **(a)** agreement **(b)** delay **(c)** struggle **(d)** enjoyment.

22. In the 1950s, Kenya was torn by some very bitter fighting. Yet a generation later Kenya was considered one of the most *stable* of the new nations.
Stable (216) means **(a)** weak and nervous **(b)** suitable for animals **(c)** bright and quick **(d)** firm and unchanging

23. "Our aim is not to select a man because he is black or brown, but on his *capability*."
Capability (216) means **(a)** new ideas **(b)** enthusiasm **(c)** ability **(d)** excitement.

24. Kenyatta disliked *pettiness* and a mean spirit.
Pettiness (216) means **(a)** charm **(b)** narrow-mindedness **(c)** wisdom **(d)** friendliness.

25. Each animal looked different. He had to know every animal in the herd by its *distinctive* markings. *Distinctive* (216) means **(a)** ugly **(b)** brown **(c)** special **(d)** branded.

THINKING IT OVER

1. Besides those mentioned in the chapter, how many of the independent nations of Africa can you name?
2. How did Kenyatta put the welfare of his country above any personal feelings he may have had?
3. Jomo Kenyatta is Kenya's founder. Who might occupy a similar place in American history? In what ways can these two people be compared?
4. As Richard Cox has pointed out in *Kenyatta's Country,* Kenya has no natural boundaries. "For the most part they follow no natural feature, no river, or escarpment [cliff], they accord with no tribal boundary." Why does this situation add to the difficulties of governing Kenya?
5. Writers and political leaders often divide the world into "industrial nations" and "developing nations." What is meant by these two terms? Most of the nations of Africa are developing nations. What special problems do they have?
6. Would you prefer to have a life with many ups and downs, with many victories and defeats, or would you like your life to be more even, more quiet and peaceful? What kind of life did Kenyatta have?

ANOTHER LOOK AT THE QUOTATION

His heart was as great as the world, but there was no room in it to hold the memory of a wrong.
RALPH WALDO EMERSON

1. Explain the quotation in your own words.
2. How does the quotation describe someone like Kenyatta? Explain.
3. Why is it foolish to hold a grudge?

WORDS AT YOUR SERVICE—METAPHOR AND SIMILE

The Lion of Kenya, as he was called, had earned respect. (220)

We are not talking about an actual lion here, but about Kenyatta. Like a lion, he was strong, proud, courageous, and worthy of respect. This is an example of *metaphor*.

Metaphor is one of the commonest things in language. Metaphor compares two basically unlike things without using *like* or *as*. If we had said Kenyatta was *like a lion*, we'd have created a simile. But we made a bolder statement and simply called Kenyatta a *lion*.

You use metaphor all the time without realizing it. You awake from a *deep* sleep, *throw* on your clothes, *gobble down* a quick breakfast, *fly out* of the house, and *catch* a bus. Throughout the day you use all kinds of metaphors like *come to* a conclusion, *fall down* (or *go up*) in your grades, *drop* your eyes, or *boil* outside in the sun.

What do the following metaphors mean?

1. It had *swallowed up* the ancient kingdom of Ghana. *Swallowed up* (215) means **(a)** visited **(b)** liked **(c)** taken over **(d)** moved away from.

2. *The winds of freedom began to blow across the face of Africa.*
   This sentence (215) means that **(a)** terrible storms began to strike Africa. **(b)** African hopes for independence would not come true **(c)** a few false leaders would arouse the people to acts of cruelty **(d)** the African people wanted to be free.
3. He *kept his head.*
   Kept his head (216) means he **(a)** was calm **(b)** remembered his enemies **(c)** gave in to the authorities **(d)** looked for wise assistants.
4. "The truth shall be known that we, as African leaders, have *stood for* peace."
   Stood for (218) means **(a)** fought against **(b)** worried about **(c)** scorned **(d)** desired.
5. Kenyatta could be called the "*father* of his country."
   Father (220) means **(a)** friend **(b)** founder **(c)** relative **(d)** outstanding person.

Jomo Kenyatta was like like a lion.

This comparison of unlike things is called a *simile*. Simile differs from metaphor. Both are comparisons, but simile is more direct, using the words *like* or *as*. Try creating some original similes. Complete each of the following.
1. as silent as . . .
2. as fleeting as . . .
3. as loud as . . .
4. as solid as . . .
5. as common as . . .

LUIS MUÑOZ MARÍN:

Puerto Rican Statesman

Strong men are made by opposition;
like kites they go up against the wind.

FRANK HARRIS

227

A few hundred miles from the southern coast of Florida lies a land of great beauty, Puerto Rico. For many years American tourists have flocked to this lovely island. They have discovered the charm of old San Juan, a city with a long history. They have toured beautiful little villages and have visited the impressive rain forest. Yet many Americans do not know much about Puerto Rico. They know little of Puerto Rico's long and colorful history. Nor are they familiar with the story of Puerto Rico's association with the United States. For nearly a century Puerto Rico and the United States have formed a partnership. The partnership has been uneasy at times, but the close ties have always remained.

Let us look more closely at the Puerto Rican story, with special notice of its statesman Luis Muñoz Marín. In Puerto Rican history Muñoz is a giant. When some people hear the name *Puerto Rico,* they think only of the musical *West Side Story.* The time has come to understand some of the problems and successes of this lovely land and its friendly people.

For hundreds of years Puerto Rico has been an important island in the Caribbean Sea. Many European powers have tried to gain control of this island, since it was at the crossroads of many trade routes.

Yet our story doesn't begin hundreds of years ago. It begins nearly 2,000 years ago. The island was probably settled by Indians from Florida. By A.D. 120 the natives had become hunters and sailors. They developed skills in making pottery. They built excellent canoes.

Waves of Indians came ashore through the years. Some tribes were peaceful. Others were fierce. The warlike Caribs often raided the island and threatened the more peaceful people living there. Later the Caribs were among the strongest enemies of the first European settlers.

The Indian influence is remembered today in many of the island's names, like *Humacao, Caguas, Mayagüez,* and *Utuado.* Our word *hammock* comes from an Indian language. The Spaniards who controlled the island borrowed many other Indian names and words.

The first European to see Puerto Rico was Christopher Columbus. On November 19, 1493, during his second voyage to the New World, he landed there and called the island San Juan Bautista (St. John the Baptist). The first permanent Spanish settlement was made in 1509. At that time, Ponce de León led a group of settlers from Hispaniola, the island that now includes the Dominican Republic and Haiti. He founded the town of Caparra, not far from the present capital of San Juan.

Almost from the beginning, Europeans brought slaves from Africa to the island. These slaves supplied important labor for mining and for agriculture. They were most useful in the sugar industry.

The economy of the islands had its ups and downs. There were periods of plenty and periods of want. Occasional epidemics, diseases that spread through the island, kept the population down.

In 1513 Ponce de León left the island to explore Florida. While he was gone, the Spaniards moved the capital from Caparra to a beautiful port nearby. They called this port Puerto Rico, which means "rich port." The name was later given to the entire island.

In the sixteenth century, Spain was the leading European power, but France and England often challenged that power. The area north of South America in the Caribbean was called the Spanish Main. Sea rovers and pirates raided ships sailing through those waters. Puerto Rico was a rich prize. These seagoing robbers often had the unofficial blessing of the French or English governments.

The first defenses of Puerto Rico were set up in 1522, but even these were poor. Ten years later the Spaniards improved their defenses with a better series of *fortifications*. In the 1540s they began construction of El Morro fortifications. These fortifications protected the capital, but the rest of Puerto Rico was open to invasion, especially by the French.

By the time the French danger had lessened, the English began their attacks. In January 1595 the English captain Sir Francis Drake attacked the island, but courageous islanders beat off the assault. In June came another attack. On *July* 1 a landing party reached the capital, San Juan. For 65 days the English occupied the island. But disease and the courageous islanders caused them to depart. In 1603 the new king of England, James I, made peace with Spain.

Puerto Rico earned a little rest. But in 1625 the Dutch attacked and landed troops in front of the fortifications. Within six weeks they, too, were defeated and left.

Spanish strength was *declining,* while English, French, and Dutch strength was increasing. Still, Puerto Rico remained a prize that was never captured by any one of the threatening powers. Puerto Ricans were developing a national pride.

In 1765 Marshall Alejandro O'Reilly named the island Puerto Rico and gave it leadership. He helped in every way. He improved the defenses. Secure, Puerto Rico's population began to grow. As time went on, Puerto Rico traded more and more with the United States.

The nineteenth century was a time of *turmoil* and unrest in Latin America. Venezuela rebelled from Spain in 1810, but the revolution was defeated. Time was on the side of the losers, however. Venezuela won independence in 1821. Other colonies soon followed. Puerto Rico, however, remained firmly under the control of Spain.

New ideas were being introduced all the time. In 1868 a great patriot, Ramón Emeterio Betances, wanted to free the slaves. He spoke up for the *abolition* of slavery. He fought for freedom of the press and other liberties. Though his first efforts failed, the later succeeded. Slavery was abolished on March 22, 1873.

In 1898 war broke out between the United States and Spain. The United States forces landed on Puerto Rico. The citizens of Ponce welcomed the Americans. The Americans stayed on and administered Puerto Rico as a territory of the United States. Spanish power in the Caribbean was ended.

People disagreed about the American presence. This was a period of sharply *conflicting* opinions. Some Puerto Ricans thought the islands were ready for immediate independence. Others thought not. Three points of view have developed through the years. One group would like to see Puerto Rico completely free and independent. A second group would like to see self-rule but with close links to the U.S. government. A third group would like to see Puerto Rico become the fifty-first state. No one group has ever had a majority.

Through the years many important steps were taken. In 1917 Puerto Ricans were declared American citizens. In 1952 a Constitution was accepted. Puerto Rico was declared a commonwealth. It has its own flag and the right to make its own laws. It can elect its own officials without the approval of the United States. Its foreign policy continues to be controlled by the American government, however.

History is made by people. One of Puerto Rico's greatest leaders was Luis Muñoz Marín. He led the country through many difficult times. His story is the story of modern Puerto Rico.

Muñoz was born in San Juan on February 18, 1898,

just before the beginning of the Spanish-American War. His father, Muñoz-Rivera, was known as the "George Washington of Puerto Rico." He had won from the Spanish some important agreements about freedom in the island. After the war, he became a commissioner in Washington. He got Congress to grant the islanders American citizenship.

Young Muñoz lived in New York City and Washington, D.C. He studied at Georgetown University. He and his father did not always see eye to eye, but they respected each other. After his father's death, Muñoz became a writer in New York and an editor. At first he urged complete independence for Puerto Rico, but years later he changed his views.

On September 13, 1928, Puerto Rico was hit by a terrible hurricane. A third of the sugar cane crop was destroyed, as was half the coffee crop. Then in 1929 nations around the world began to suffer hard times. Because of the hurricane, Puerto Rico may have suffered more than most.

Muñoz returned to Puerto Rico in 1931 to stay. He was a firm believer in democracy and a friend of the peasant. He was elected senator in the Puerto Rican Legislature in 1932, but there were bad times ahead. The island suffered from a period of hard times called the Great Depression. Wages fell. Many people were thrown out of work. Businesses closed. People went hungry. People throughout the world suffered, but Puerto Rico was especially hard hit.

Something had to be done. Luis Muñoz Marín led the way. He played a role in the New Deal, a program begun by President Franklin D. Roosevelt. He was a friend of Roosevelt's wife, Eleanor. He called on her for help.

Mrs. Roosevelt visited the island in March 1934 and went into the poor districts. She realized that Puerto

Rico wanted real help, not just temporary relief. In a 1943 speech, Muñoz said Puerto Rico needed "more vitamins and less aspirin." He made a firm effort to improve the island's economy.

In 1936 Millard Tydings, a United States senator, backed a bill to grant complete independence to Puerto Rico. Muñoz, who had once sought independence, now opposed it. He felt that the United States and Puerto Rico could work together to bring the island out of the depression. In August 1947, Congress granted Puerto Rico the right to elect its own governor. Muñoz was elected the following year. He held the post until 1965.

Soon after World War II he helped organize "Operation Bootstrap." The plan provided tax advantages to businesses. Factories began to spring up. All kinds of products were made: nylon, shoes, lenses, and electrical equipment. The program set up over 2,300 new factories. It also expanded agriculture, transportation, and communication. Puerto Rico now has one of the highest standards of living in Latin America.

Muñoz was very close to John F. Kennedy. Even before he became president, Kennedy showed an interest in Puerto Rico. In a speech in December 1958, he paid tribute to Muñoz. He said America needed leadership, "leadership such as that which you have achieved in Puerto Rico . . . which our nation needs today in both domestic and foreign affairs." After his election, President Kennedy remained interested in the island.

In 1963 Muñoz received the Presidential Medal of Freedom. He continued to be an important person in Puerto Rican affairs, but his period of governorship was ending. In 1964 a younger man, Luis A. Ferré, was elected governor.

In 1967 the people voted to continue as a commonwealth. Since then there have been strong voices heard on every side. Puerto Rico is free to decide its own fate, but most people prefer the commonwealth arrangement.

In 1976 Muñoz was co-chairman of a group studying Puerto Rico's condition. Many groups have studied the situation and many have recommended changes. Presidents Gerald Ford and Ronald Reagan have spoken out for statehood. Some Puerto Ricans have agreed. Other Puerto Ricans have urged complete independence. The majority of the people, however, seem to favor a middle position.

On April 30, 1980, Muñoz Marín died. He had been in poor health for years. To the end of his life, he had one dream. He wanted to strengthen the commonwealth idea. He felt that that was the best way for Puerto Rico to be associated with the United States. But he also wanted to preserve Puerto Rico's rich culture. The Puerto Rican language, literature, and arts are a treasure worth preserving.

Luis Muñoz Marín made his contribution toward that goal.

UNDERSTANDING WHAT YOU HAVE READ

Finding Another Title

1. Another good title for this selection might be **(a)** The Long and Colorful History of the Caribbean **(b)** How the United States and Puerto Rico Have Learned to Live Together **(c)** The Story of the "George Washington" of Puerto Rico **(d)** The Story of Puerto Rico and a Great Leader.

Getting the Main Idea

2. Throughout their history, Puerto Ricans have **(a)** shown courage, determination, and pride **(b)** failed to keep the Spanish language alive **(c)** chosen leaders who have not understood their problems **(d)** traded with nearly every country in the world.

Finding Details

3. The Indians who settled Puerto Rico probably came from **(a)** Hispaniola **(b)** Florida **(c)** Venezuela **(d)** Cuba.
4. Columbus first came to Puerto Rico in **(a)** 1492 **(b)** 1493 **(c)** 1494 **(d)** 1508.
5. When Ponce de León left the island in 1513, **(a)** the Carib Indians revolted **(b)** Sir Francis Drake attacked **(c)** the Spaniards moved the capital **(d)** San Juan Bautista landed on the island.
6. The Spanish Main was **(a)** part of the Caribbean **(b)** a Spanish warship **(c)** a treasure of jewels and gold **(d)** in the mountains of Venezuela.
7. European nations attacked Puerto Rico in the following order **(a)** Dutch, French, English **(b)** French, Dutch, English **(c)** English, French, Dutch **(d)** French, English, Dutch.
8. Marshall O'Reilly **(a)** was an Irish sea captain **(b)** led the English forces **(c)** was an able Puerto Rican leader **(d)** was an American soldier who landed on Puerto Rico.
9. Muñoz Marín went to Puerto Rico to stay in **(a)** 1928 **(b)** 1929 **(c)** 1931 **(d)** 1932.
10. The American president who was closest to Muñoz was **(a)** John F. Kennedy **(b)** Richard Nixon **(c)** Gerald Ford **(d)** Ronald Reagan.

Making Inferences

11. The early Spanish settlers on Puerto Rico probably (a) were mostly merchants and business people (b) learned a great deal about agriculture from the Indians (c) discovered a great deal of gold in the Puerto Rican mines (d) gave up Spanish and learned to talk mostly in an Indian language.

12. The islanders were able to beat back the invading Dutch, French, and English because (a) they had better guns (b) of their courage in defending their homeland (c) of a sudden hurricane (d) they had help from South America.

13. Muñoz probably changed his views about complete independence for Puerto Rico when he (a) became a writer in New York (b) studied at Georgetown University (c) realized that the United States could help Puerto Rico (d) was an editor in New York City.

14. Muñoz believed that to help the people, Puerto Rico (a) would have to become the fifty-first state (b) should reduce the number of factories to end pollution (c) should once again be part of Spain (d) would have to build more factories.

15. "Operation Bootstrap" could be considered (a) of little help (b) a complete failure (c) a strange idea (d) a success.

Predicting What Happens Next

16. After the death of Muñoz, Puerto Ricans probably (a) honored him (b) quickly forgot him (c) gave up the programs he started (d) asked that he be buried in the United States.

Deciding on the Order of Events

17. The following events are scrambled. Arrange them in proper order, as they happened. Use letters only.
    (a) Ramón Emeterio Betances fights for freedom.
    (b) Ponce de León founds the city of Caparra.
    (c) The Spanish-American War breaks out.
    (d) Luis Muñoz Marín becomes governor of Puerto Rico.

Inferring Attitude

18. When John F. Kennedy spoke about Muñoz (233), he was (a) humorous (b) sincere (c) uninterested (d) nasty.

Separating Facts from Opinions

For each of the following, tell whether the statement is a fact *(F)* or an opinion *(O)*.

19. Muñoz was the greatest leader in Puerto Rican history.
20. Puerto Rico should become the fifty-first state.

Understanding Words from Context

21. Ten years later the Spaniards improved their defenses with a better series of *fortifications*.
    Fortifications (230) are structures used for (a) breaking through enemy lines (b) providing homes for nurses and doctors (c) security against attack (d) displaying the wealth and strength of a country.

22. Spanish strength was *declining,* while English, French, and Dutch strength was increasing.
    Declining (230) means **(a)** lessening **(b)** growing **(c)** exploding **(d)** happening.
23. The nineteenth century was a time of *turmoil* and unrest in Latin America.
    Turmoil (230) means **(a)** plenty **(b)** fun **(c)** good action **(d)** confusion.
24. In 1868, a great patriot, Ramón Emeterio Betances, wanted to free the slaves. He spoke up for the *abolition* of slavery.
    Abolition (231) means **(a)** promotion **(b)** ending **(c)** advertising **(d)** understanding.
25. People disagreed about the American presence. This was a period of sharply *conflicting* opinions.
    Conflicting (231) means **(a)** lively **(b)** disagreeing **(c)** unsound **(d)** emotional.

UNDERSTANDING WHAT YOU HAVE READ

1. Why was Puerto Rico considered so important to European nations?
2. How did the Puerto Ricans show their courage time after time?
3. How did Muñoz help build Puerto Rico?
4. Why did Muñoz change his mind later about the complete independence of Puerto Rico?
5. What are the three main points of view about the future of Puerto Rico? Which point of view do most Puerto Ricans seem to hold? Which point of view do you hold?
6. Why is it a good thing for Puerto Ricans to keep their language and arts alive?

7. Many Puerto Ricans have moved to the United States. Their language is Spanish. Should English be officially adopted as the language of the United States? Should all public signs be in English? Tell how you feel.
8. Why is it important to know something about the history and culture of Puerto Rico?

ANOTHER LOOK AT THE QUOTATION

> *Strong men are made by opposition;*
> *like kites they go up against the wind.*
>
> FRANK HARRIS

1. Explain the quotation in your own words.
2. Has the quotation been proved true in your own life? How?
3. What problems did Muñoz have to face in trying to help his people? Was he probably made strong by opposition?

WORDS AT YOUR SERVICE—WORDS FROM NAMES

> *On July 1 a landing party reached the*
> *capital, San Juan. (230)*

July is a good illustration of certain kinds of English words. Such words have been formed from proper names. *July,* for example, is named for *Julius* Ceasar, who is given credit for an improved calendar. *August* is named for *Augustus* Caesar, first emperor of Rome.

January is named for *Janus,* the god of doors. He is usually pictured with two faces. At the beginning of the new year, January faces back at the old year and forward to the new.

Sunday and *Monday* are named for the sun and moon, but the other days are named for Norse and Roman gods. *Saturday,* for example, is *Saturn's day.* Wednesday is *Woden's day.*

Many everyday words have their origin in proper names. *China* for dishes and *cashmere* for wool are named for places in Asia. The fruit *tangerine* is named for *Tangier,* in Africa. The flowers *magnolia, gardenia, forsythia,* and *zinnia* are named for people.

Below are ten words with the person the word was named for. Using this information, complete each sentence after the list with the correct word.

braille	Louis Braille was blinded as a child, but his father made sure the boy had a good education.
cardigan	The earl of Cardigan was a soldier who wore a special woolen vest to protect himself against the winter in Russia.
fahrenheit	Gabriel Daniel Fahrenheit made the first usable mercury thermometer. He also invented the scale for measuring temperature.
Levis	Levi Strauss was a pioneer overall manufacturer from San Francisco. He used copper rivets in his heavy blue denim pants to make them stronger.
macadam	John Loudon Macadam was interested in road improvement. He invented a way of constructing good, economical roads.

pasteurized	Louis Pasteur experimented with keeping milk from spoiling through the use of heat.
tantalized	In Greek mythology Tantalus was punished in the afterlife by standing in water up to his chin. Above his head were choice fruits, just out of reach. When he dipped his head to drink, the water went away. When he reached for the fruit, he couldn't quite get any.
titanic	In Greek mythology, the Titans were giants.
vandalism	In A.D. 455 the Vandals captured Rome and carried off many treasures. Later they were accused of senselessly destroying works of art.
vulcanized	In Roman mythology Vulcan was the god of fire.

1. When you are in doubt, drink milk that has been ———— rather than raw milk.
2. Some gardens have identifying signs written in ———— to help those who cannot see but who can enjoy the fragrance.
3. Nathaniel knitted Marie a ———— to keep her warm during the chilly San Antonio winter.
4. Seeing all that delicious food on television ———— me, especially since I couldn't get any.
5. An earthquake of 8 on the Richter scale is very dangerous; it is ————.
6. Don't dress too formally for the party. Wear your ————.
7. On the ———— scale 212 degrees is the boiling point of water at sea level. On the Celsius scale it is 100.

8. I'll be so happy when they turn our dirt-and-gravel road into a hard-top ——— road.
9. I think that hole in the inner tube can be ——— and repaired.
10. Senseless ———, the destruction of property, helps no one and hurts many.

COMPLETING AN OUTLINE

The article on Luis Muñoz Marín might be outlined in the following way. Five outline items have been omitted. Test your understanding of the structure of the article by following the directions after the outline.

I. Puerto Rico—a history
    A.
    B. Arrival of Spaniards
    C. Attacks by French, English, Dutch
    D. Independence of other Spanish colonies
    E. Leaders in the nineteenth century

II. Puerto Rico and the United States
    A. Arrival of U.S. forces
    B.
    C. The Constitution

III. Luis Muñoz Marín as leader
    A.
    B. Concern for peasants
    C. Belief in democracy
    D. Election as first governor
    E. Honors and awards

IV. Operation Bootstrap
    A. Hard times in Puerto Rico
    B.
    C. Improvement in economy

V. Later events
    A. Studies of Puerto Rico's situation
    B. Three major points of view
    C.

Fill in the items omitted from the outline. Correctly match the items in column A with the outline numbers in column B.

A	B
1. Death of Muñoz	**a.** I. A.
2. Indian cultures	**b.** II. B.
3. Increase in factories	**c.** III. A.
4. Early experiences in the United States	**d.** IV. B.
5. Grant of American citizenship	**e.** V. C.

HOW MUCH DO YOU REMEMBER?

1. *Operation Bootstrap* was a plan used in **(a)** China **(b)** Kenya **(c)** Puerto Rico **(d)** Lebanon.
2. Falling windows seriously damaged the career of **(a)** Frank Lloyd Wright **(b)** Louis Sullivan **(c)** Walter Gropius **(d)** I. M. Pei.
3. The Kennedy library was designed by **(a)** William Zechendorf **(b)** Edward Durrell Stone **(c)** I. M. Pei **(d)** Jacqueline Kennedy.
4. The person who was at one time imprisoned by the British is **(a)** Jomo Kenyatta **(b)** Idi Amin **(c)** the father of Muñoz Marín **(d)** Millard Tydings.
5. John F. Kennedy was a close friend of **(a)** Ramón Emeterio Betances **(b)** Luis Muñoz Marín **(c)** Jomo Kenyatta **(d)** Anwar el-Sadat.
6. Greek Revival is a **(a)** style of architecture **(b)** religious awakening **(c)** method of saving drowning people **(d)** group of Greek immigrants in the United States.
7. Groups of Puerto Ricans suggest all the following for the future of their homeland EXCEPT **(a)** statehood **(b)** complete independence **(c)** keeping the commonwealth arrangement **(d)** union with Cuba.

8. Americans tend to be (a) deeply interested in the new nations of West Africa (b) ignorant about Africa (c) opposed to Jomo Kenyatta's policies (d) in favor of a high-speed rail line from Cairo to Cape Town.

9. The Louvre is a famous art museum in (a) Montreal (b) Denver (c) Paris (d) New Delhi.

10. A phrase that might best describe Jomo Kenyatta is (a) enemy of the British (b) cruel leader (c) lover of peace (d) unreliable friend.

WHAT IS YOUR OPINION?

1. How did Muñoz Marín and Jomo Kenyatta resemble each other? Which one of them seems to you the best leader? Why?

2. What is the latest news from Africa? Are there encouraging signs?

3. What, in your opinion, are some of the outstanding monuments and buildings in the United States?

4. Should the United States take a greater interest in the nations of Africa? Explain.

5. Why can leaders not always do as they would like to do? What are some of the problems all leaders face?

THE QUOTATION AND THE UNIT

> *The higher you climb on the mountain,*
> *the harder the wind blows.*
>
> SAM CUMMINGS

1. Explain the quotation in your own words.
2. What comparison is the speaker making? Is it a good comparison? Why?
3. Why do all leaders receive criticism?
4. Does the quotation hold true for people other than leaders? Why is there so much pressure on the number-one tennis player, for example? Why do the outstanding quarterback in football and the leading home-run hitter in baseball experience so much tension?

UNIT 5

ARCHITECTS OF THE FUTURE

Steady nerves and a quiet mind are not things we go out and find; they are things we create.

JOHN R. MILLER

You'll live the rest of your life in the future. What kind of future will it be? What forces will decide what you'll do and how you'll live?

The three subjects in this unit are working in ways to affect that future. Each in his or her own way is setting a direction, nudging the world along the way it should go.

Margaret Thatcher, prime minister of Great Britain, has shown that a woman can lead a Western democracy. She has broken a long-standing, unwritten rule that only a man can be prime minister of Great Britain. She has shown that a woman can be as strong, as determined, and as intelligent as a man in

247

handling the difficulties that face every nation.

Andrew Young has held many jobs in his life. His election to Congress demonstrated that doors of opportunity are opening for all. His assignment as U.S. ambassador to the United Nations showed the world that the United States is growing up. He proved that a person's color is becoming less important in the United States.

Mother Teresa has shown that one woman can make a difference in fighting poverty and disease. She has brought hope and good health to thousands of people who might otherwise have been forgotten. She has stirred the conscience of the world and looked toward a better world in years to come.

All three subjects, in different ways, show the world we might have someday, with equal opportunities for all.

MARGARET THATCHER:

British Prime Minister

*Keep your fears to yourself, but share
your courage with others.*
ROBERT LOUIS STEVENSON

Trouble was brewing. For many years Argentina had laid claim to the Falkland Islands. These lonely islands in the South Atlantic hold only about 1,800 settlers. All the people living there are British who wish to remain British. The islands are not wealthy. The chief industry is raising sheep. The chief export is wool.

The Malvinas, as they are named in Spanish, do not seem to be valuable enough to be cause for war. But in the spring of 1982, war did break out. The struggle matched the nearby South American nation, Argentina, against a European industrial power, Great Britain. The Falklands are only 250 miles from Argentina but 8,000 miles from Great Britain.

Before the war, talks had gone on for years between Argentina and Great Britain. These fell through. On March 20, Argentine civilians came ashore on South Georgia Island. This was the beginning of war. On April 2, several thousand Argentine soldiers invaded the main island. Two days later Argentina announced that its forces controlled the island.

There were attempts to stop the invasion. The United Nations Security Council demanded the removal of Argentine troops. The Argentines ignored this demand. Alexander Haig, the American secretary of state, tried to get a settlement between the two powers. He failed.

Three days after the invasion, Great Britain sent a naval force to the Falklands. Soldiers were put aboard ships and sent to the battle zone. They had a long way to go. Argentina sent at least 8,000 troops to hold the islands.

On April 25, the British recaptured the principal port on South Georgia Island. On April 30 President Ronald Reagan accused Argentina of "armed aggression" and sided with Great Britain.

The naval warfare *intensified,* as the two navies

clashed. An Argentine cruiser was sunk on May 3. A British destroyer was sunk on May 4. The British set up a naval blockade that hurt the Argentine cause.

On May 14, a large force of British soldiers arrived at the islands. The *Queen Elizabeth II,* usually used for carrying tourists, had become a troop carrier. On May 21 thousands of British troops came ashore and began fighting their way across the island.

The end was no longer in doubt. The British controlled the seas. On June 14 the Argentine troops began to surrender. On June 15 Prime Minister Margaret Thatcher announced that the war was over. Two days later the Argentine president, General Leopoldo Galtieri, resigned as commander in chief of his country.

Who was this woman who had led Great Britain through ten very difficult weeks? Margaret Thatcher proved that a woman leader could be as strong as any man. She proved that in a *crisis,* a woman could weather the storm. Some people were amazed at her *unconquerable* spirit. But those who knew her were not surprised at her show of strength. Anyone who had followed her career knew that Margaret Thatcher could meet problems head on.

Margaret Hilda Roberts was born in an apartment above the family grocery store on October 13, 1925. Her father was active in the politics of her hometown, Grantham. In this market town about 100 miles north of London, young Margaret received a sound education.

Margaret's father was a great believer in education. As she said in an interview: "I always got the books I wanted but no pleasures. I never went to a dance until I got to university."

Margaret *excelled* in school, standing out among her classmates. She skipped a grade in elementary school and won a scholarship to Grantham Girls' School at the age of ten. (A *scholarship* is a grant of money.) Although she was a year younger than her fellow students, she was usually at the head of her class. She was also a fine athlete. Shortly before graduation she was named the outstanding girl by her teachers.

During her vacations she helped out in the grocery store. In her spare time she began a hobby that changed her life. She read all about politics and international affairs. At one time her father was a judge in the community. Margaret sat in on his court sessions and learned a great deal about the law and politics.

In 1935 she had her first taste of politics. As a ten-year-old she ran errands for the Conservative party in her district. She became a lifelong Conservative.

Margaret won a scholarship to Oxford University, where she studied chemistry. She could not forget her interest in politics, however. In 1946 she was elected president of the Oxford University Conservative Association.

After she got her degree in natural science in 1947, she took a job as a research chemist. But her heart was really elsewhere. She attended a Conservative party conference in 1949. She impressed the chairman of the organization so much that he asked her to run for election to Parliament, the British *counterpart* of our Congress. She was a Conservative running against a Labour party candidate.

She made a good showing but did not win this first time. She got 36 percent of the vote in an area strongly held by the Labour party. She ran again two years later and won 40 percent of the vote. At this time she met and married Denis Thatcher.

In 1951 Margaret began to study law in her spare time. She passed the bar exam and practiced law. She still had her eye on the political scene. She ran for election in a different district in 1959. She won easily and took her seat among the 365 Conservative members of the House of Commons in Parliament.

In her first term she made an impression by introducing a bill that was later passed. In 1961 Prime Minister Harold Macmillan gave her a job as secretary in charge of pensions. Her understanding of the problem and of people impressed her fellow members.

In 1964 the Labour party came to power. Margaret Thatcher became a strong member of the *opposition,* the party out of power. She rose even higher in her party. When the Conservatives returned to power in 1970, Margaret Thatcher was ready. She became secretary of state for education and science. This was a major task for her.

These were stormy years for Margaret Thatcher. She did many things, some of them unpopular. But even her opponents recognized her sincerity. She was willing to accept short-term losses for long-term gains.

As in all true democracies, power seesaws from one party to another. In 1974 the Labour party came back into power. Once again Thatcher became an important opposition leader. She remained very much in the public eye. She did not always hold popular views, but she presented her ideas with force.

During this period the leader of the Conservative party was Edward Heath. Many members criticized him for leading the Conservatives to defeat in three elections out of four. Thatcher noted the party's unhappiness with Heath. She kept her eye on party leadership.

On February 4, 1975, Thatcher challenged Heath. She received 130 votes against his 119. A third candidate received 16 votes. To have a majority, a candidate must receive more than half of the votes. Since no one had a majority, another election was held. This time Thatcher won a clear victory.

Margaret Thatcher had done something almost unbelievable. A woman, she had defeated the strongest man in her party. The political system of Great Britain had seldom seen a woman in the higher circles of power. Margaret Thatcher was nearly at the top. As leader of the opposition, she had a chance to become prime minister someday.

She appointed people to posts on the basis of ability. She did not favor any special group in her party. As the reporter Anthony Shrimsley said, "Even those opposed to Mrs. Thatcher are beginning to realize that . . . she is not allowing herself to be captured by any group."

Thatcher was a hard fighter during this period when her party was out of power. She did not have too long to wait. The Conservatives rode into power in May 1979. Margaret Thatcher became prime minister on May 4.

The years after she took office were difficult ones. A glance at the newspapers during the 1980s will show Thatcher's name on almost every front page. This was a time of problems at home and abroad. She had to make all kinds of day-to-day decisions that would test the will of anyone.

Rapidly rising prices were troubling the nations of the West. The threat of atomic war called for hard decisions. Unemployment rose to dangerous levels.

Her popularity had its ups and downs. When she successfully led the nation in the Falklands War, she was very popular. But when she had to make some hard choices on the home front, she lost some of that popularity. Through every difficulty, she has always been a friend of the United States.

Strikes are always a problem for leaders. A coal strike early in her leadership was settled quickly. Then came a more serious threat. On March 12, 1984, a great many coal miners walked out. This time she refused to budge.

The strike dragged on and on. Finally, the miners went back to work without having their demands met. This made her popular with some, unpopular with others.

She often had to meet with world leaders. In 1984, for example, she met with President Reagan, French President François Mitterrand, and Russian leader Mikhail Gorbachev.

By 1985 there were signs of discontent in the Conservative party. No democratic leader stays in power forever. There were signs that Thatcher might be removed from power. But whatever the future held, Margaret Thatcher would keep her place in history.

What is Margaret Thatcher like personally? She can be a strong leader. She doesn't give up easily. She is also a warm human being. She has two children, Mark and Carol. She and her husband have a town house in London and a country apartment in Kent. She enjoys being cook, housekeeper, and hostess. She collects art objects. She enjoys the opera and music festivals.

She looks much younger than her years. She has a slight build and "piercing blue eyes." She also has a keen sense of humor. She once said, "In politics, if you want anything said, ask a man; if you want anything done, ask a woman."

UNDERSTANDING WHAT YOU HAVE READ

Finding Another Title

1. Another good title for this selection might be **(a)** Politics in England **(b)** How the Conservatives Defeated the Labour Party **(c)** A Political Leader with Courage **(d)** How to Win an Election.

Getting the Main Idea

2. Margaret Thatcher (a) has devoted her life to politics (b) failed as a political leader (c) did not show much promise in school (d) is a devoted wife and mother.

Finding Details

3. The Malvinas (a) are leaders of Argentina (b) are islands in the South Atlantic (c) belong to Argentina (d) are located inside Argentina.
4. The *Queen Elizabeth II* is the name of a passenger ship used as (a) an aircraft carrier (b) a battle ship (c) an armored tank (d) a troop ship.
5. Margaret Thatcher's father was (a) a retired naval officer (b) a policeman (c) active in politics (d) a teacher.
6. Margaret won a scholarship, or grant, at the age of (a) eight (b) ten (c) 12 (d) 14.
7. When Margaret sat in on court sessions, the judge was (a) Harold Macmillan (b) Denis Thatcher (c) her uncle (d) her father.
8. As her first assignment after she was elected to the House of Commons, she was (a) secretary in charge of pensions (b) assistant to Edward Heath (c) secretary of state for education and science (d) none of these.
9. Two years during which the Labour party returned to power were (a) 1961 and 1964 (b) 1964 and 1970 (c) 1970 and 1974 (d) 1964 and 1974.
10. Margaret Thatcher met with each of the following leaders EXCEPT (a) Mikhail Gorbachev (b) Leopoldo Galtieri (c) François Mitterrand (d) Ronald Reagan.

Making Inferences

11. The British won their first victory against the Argentines on **(a)** April 2 **(b)** April 25 **(c)** April 30 **(d)** May 3.

12. Probably a major reason for the Argentine defeat was **(a)** Britain's control of the sea and the naval blockade **(b)** The closeness of the Falklands to Argentina **(c)** the demands of the United Nations **(d)** Alexander Haig's trips to solve the problem.

13. Thatcher lost her first election because **(a)** she did not campaign hard enough **(b)** her friends deserted her **(c)** she was running in a Labour stronghold **(d)** she wasn't really interested in getting the job.

14. Thatcher **(a)** is generally true to her principles **(b)** doesn't like a good fight **(c)** is often uncertain in her decisions **(d)** never loses.

15. In choosing people for important posts, Margaret Thatcher did NOT **(a)** make good choices **(b)** let friendship influence her decision **(c)** stand by people she chose **(d)** think seriously about her choices.

Predicting What Happens Next

16. When Thatcher and her Conservatives came to power, the Labour party members **(a)** asked her for jobs **(b)** were secretly happy **(c)** decided to become Conservatives **(d)** felt free to attack her actions.

Deciding on the Order of Events

17. The following events are scrambled. Arrange them in proper order, as they happened. Use letters only.

(a) Margaret marries Denis Thatcher.
(b) Thatcher becomes prime minister.
(c) Argentina invades the Falkland Islands.
(d) Margaret wins a scholarship to Grantham Girls' School.

Inferring Attitude

18. When Margaret Thatcher said (255), "If you want anything done, ask a woman," she was speaking (a) cruelly (b) seriously (c) jokingly (d) unhappily.

Separating Facts from Opinions

For each of the following, tell whether the statement is a fact (*F*) or an opinion (*O*).

19. Margaret Thatcher's work makes her one of the most outstanding women of the last ten years.

20. Margaret Thatcher was the major reason for the British victory in the Falkland Islands.

Understanding Words from Context

21. The naval warfare *intensified,* as the two navies clashed.
   Intensified (250) means (a) was well reported (b) got stronger (c) was forgotten (d) decreased.

22. She proved that in a *crisis,* a woman could weather the storm.
   Crisis (251) means (a) disappointment (b) unexpected moment (c) happy situation (d) dangerous time.

23. Margaret *excelled* in school, standing out among her classmates.

Excelled (251) means **(a)** did very well **(b)** attended regularly **(c)** played a musical instrument **(d)** chose her career.

24. She impressed the chairman of the organization so much that he asked her to run for election to Parliament, the British *counterpart* of our Congress.

Counterpart (252) means **(a)** government officer **(b)** legal system **(c)** similar thing **(d)** member.

25. Margaret Thatcher became a strong member of the *opposition*, the party out of power.

Opposition (253) means **(a)** a force against another force **(b)** the political party running the country **(c)** a partnership of people with different points of view **(d)** a force supporting another force.

THINKING IT OVER

1. How did Margaret Thatcher strike a blow for women in politics?
2. In 1984 Geraldine Ferraro ran for vice-president of the United States. Would you like to see a woman run for president? Why or why not?
3. Why is it impossible in a democracy for one party to stay in power forever?
4. In some elections barely half the people bother to vote. Is this lack of interest a threat to democracy? Explain.
5. Most new citizens do get out and vote. Why?
6. In Great Britain the most important person is the prime minister, who is chosen by a political party.

In the United States the president is chosen by the people. Which is a better way of choosing a leader? Explain your point of view.

7. Why do you suppose Great Britain bothered to fight an expensive war for poor islands so far from home?

8. "She was willing to accept short-term losses for long-term gains." What does this sentence mean to you? Do you agree that such a way is wise? Explain.

ANOTHER LOOK AT THE QUOTATION

Keep your fears to yourself, but share your courage with others.
ROBERT LOUIS STEVENSON

1. Explain the quotation in your own words.

2. Did Margaret Thatcher share her courage with others? Explain.

3. How may sharing fear lead to panic?

4. During World War II Winston Churchill never showed fear. How did his attitude help his people?

5. Shortly after taking office in 1932, President Franklin D. Roosevelt said, "The only thing we have to fear is fear itself." What did he mean? Why might a leader want to keep citizens from being afraid of the future?

WORDS AT YOUR SERVICE—WORDS WITHIN WORDS

Some people were amazed at her uncon-querable *spirit.*

Unconquerable is a big word, but it is not a hard word. Right in the heart of the long word is the familiar word *conquer,* to *overcome. Un* is a familiar prefix meaning *not,* as in *unwilling, unkind,* and *uncertain. Able* is a familiar suffix meaning *able to.* Putting all the ingredients together gives you *not able to be overcome,* a good definition of *unconquerable.*

When you come across a long, hard word, examine it. See whether it contains within it some easier, more familiar word. Then make a good guess, also using all the context clues you have already learned.

Try your skill at guessing meanings of longer words. Match a meaning in column B with a word in column A.

A	B
1. beautification	**a.** without weakness
2. cancellation	**b.** process of making attractive
3. centralization	**c.** not fully developed; childish
4. divisible	**d.** state of being disloyal
5. faithlessness	**e.** able to be split
6. faultless	**f.** organization under one control
7. immature	trol
8. imperfection	**g.** the act of crossing out
9. indefensible	**h.** unable to be defended
10. unreasonable	**i.** showing little sense
	j. weakness

COMPLETING AN OUTLINE

The article on Margaret Thatcher might be outlined in the following way. Five outline items have been omitted.

Test your understanding of the structure of the article by following the directions after the outline.

I. War in the Falklands
   A. Argentine invasion
   B. British response
   C.
   D. Announcement of victory by Prime Minister Thatcher

II. Margaret Thatcher's roots
   A.
   B. Interest in politics
   C. Early political defeats
   D. Marriage to Denis Thatcher

III. Margaret Thatcher on the way up
   A. Study of law
   B.
   C. Strong member of opposition
   D. Challenge to Heath
   E. Victory within the party

IV. Leadership of Conservative party
   A. Clever use of power
   B.
   C. Trials and victories
   D. A look ahead

V. Margaret Thatcher the woman
   A. Love of family
   B. Appearance
   C.

Fill in the items omitted from the outline. Correctly match the items in column A with the outline numbers in column B.

A   **B**

A	**B**
1. Appointment as prime minister	a. I. C.
2. Birth and schooling	b. II. A.
3. Sense of humor	c. III. B.
4. Surrender of Argentine forces	d. IV. B.
5. Election to Parliament	e. V. C.

ANDREW YOUNG, JR.:

Political Leader and Statesman

I have a dream that one day on the red hills of Georgia, the sons of former slaves and the sons of former slave-owners will be able to sit together at the table of brotherhood.

MARTIN LUTHER KING, JR.

Some people seem to live several lifetimes in one. They somehow cram into their time on earth many roles. They seem defeated one moment. Then the next moment they rise up and reach greater heights than before. Such a person is Andrew Young, Jr.

Many American political leaders are well known in the United States. Far fewer are known *internationally*. Andrew Young is not only a big name on the American scene. He is known far and wide as a representative of the United States. How did he achieve such widespread notice? This is his story.

Andrew Jackson Young, Jr., was born in New Orleans, Louisiana, on March 12, 1932. His father was a well-to-do dentist. His mother, Daisy Fuller Young, was a teacher. As the son of well-educated parents, Andrew had many advantages. He was raised in a middle-class neighborhood where people expected their children to succeed.

Andrew learned to read and write before he went to school. He was always an outstanding student. He graduated from Gilbert Academy in 1947 and enrolled at Dillard University in New Orleans. A year later he transferred to Howard University in Washington, D.C.

At first Andrew planned to become a dentist. He actually obtained a bachelor of science degree in 1951, but then he had second thoughts. He wanted to do something to improve the world. He hoped to become an architect of the future. He decided to enter the ministry.

He enrolled in the Hartford Theological Seminary in Hartford, Connecticut. There he was influenced by the teachings of Mahatma Gandhi, a great Indian leader. Gandhi believed in nonviolent protest. After studying Gandhi's teachings, Young became convinced that he, Andrew Young, could, as he put it, "change this country without violence."

In 1955 Young graduated with a bachelor of divinity

degree, which is a degree in religion. He was appointed a minister in a church with a largely white population. Then he returned to the South and became a minister in Marion, Alabama, and in Thomasville and Beachton, Georgia.

He was asked why he chose to return to poor churches in the South. He replied, "I wanted to be around plain, wise, black folk. I thought, then, that poor people who knew suffering and love and God could save the world."

Young became active in the civil-rights movement. Under his leadership, members of his church formed community-action groups. He helped increase black voter registration in the South. In 1957 he took still another job. He was hired by the National Council of Churches and moved to New York City. There he worked mostly with white youths. He was an associate director of the department of youth work.

Because of his excellent work, the church officials asked him to lead a voter-education drive. During the course of this project, he often worked with Dr. Martin Luther King, Jr., the leader of the most powerful civil-rights group.

With other black leaders, Young helped to draw up the Civil Rights Act of 1964 and the Voting Rights Act of 1965. He helped train many black leaders who have since become sheriffs or mayors. He also worked with white leaders to end *segregation,* the forced separation of one race from another.

After Dr. King was assassinated in April 1968, Ralph David Abernathy took over the leadership of Dr. King's civil-rights group. Abernathy named Young his first assistant. Together they planned various projects to help the civil-rights movement.

Andrew Young believed "the power in America is in the political structure." He decided to run for the U.S.

House of Representatives from a mostly white district in Georgia. He said then, "If a white majority elects a black man to Congress, it will say that the American dream is still possible and it will restore faith in this country and in the political process for a lot of people." When you restore faith, you give it back to people or set it up again.

Young won the primary election against a black opponent and two white opponents. Primary elections decide who will run as the party's candidate. Unfortunately Young was defeated in the November election. But he had started something he would finish. Two years later he ran for Congress again. This time he won. Andrew Young was a pioneer. He paved the way for others. Since Young's election, many black candidate have run for Congress in white districts—and won.

The voters approved of his efforts. Two years later he won a *landslide* victory of 72 percent. Two years after that he won by an even greater margin: 80 percent.

Young was a faithful new member of Congress. He was especially helpful to the poor and unemployed. He was also interested in the environment. He voted for programs that would protect the land from destructive mining practices.

Then came difficulties in the White House. Spiro Agnew, the vice-president of the United States, was accused of wrongdoing while he was governor of Maryland. On October 10, 1973, he resigned, and a new vice-president had to be chosen. Gerald Ford, a Republican, was nominated. Young, a Democrat, would either have to support the nomination or speak out against it. To the surprise of nearly everyone, Young supported Ford. As he said later, "Gerald Ford had voted against everything I had been for, yet I found being around him a good experience." He thought Ford deserved a chance. He proved that he believed in a man, not a label.

In the following months, the president of the United States, Richard Nixon, had problems of his own. On June 17, 1972, some of his helpers had broken into the offices of the Democratic National Committee in the Watergate office buildings in Washington. At first, not many people took the break-in too seriously. But as time went on, some of President Nixon's closest advisers were accused of cooperating with the convicted criminals.

Then President Nixon himself got into trouble. He was accused of helping to cover up the link between the White House staff and the criminals. There was danger that Congress might remove him from office. As a result, he resigned from the presidency on August 9, 1974.

Former President Nixon's troubles were not over, though. He could still be charged with a crime. On September 8, 1974, Gerald Ford, who had become president on Nixon's resignation, pardoned Richard Nixon. Many people thought Ford's action was wrong. Andrew Young thought it was right. He was the only black member of Congress who defended President Ford's pardon of Richard Nixon. Young proved that he would follow his own beliefs, not the beliefs of any political party or group.

When Jimmy Carter campaigned for the governorship of Georgia in 1970, he met Andrew Young. Carter was impressed by the younger man and often asked for his advice. When Carter ran for the presidency in 1976, Young supported him. He delivered a speech for Carter at the Democratic National Convention in July. He *emphasized* Carter's achievements in civil rights and stressed his concern for blacks.

Carter was elected in November 1976. Soon after, he chose Young to represent the United States at a meeting of American and African leaders in Lesotho, South Africa. The meeting resulted in an entirely new role for Andrew Young, who had already played many roles.

On December 16, 1976, President Carter nominated Young for the post of American ambassador to the United Nations. This is the kind of assignment that takes people from the local news pages to the world's headlines. At first Young hesitated. He would have to give up his national role. But he would be able to help form foreign plans. Young agreed to take the job.

When a person is nominated for an important job like an ambassador, the Senate must approve the nomination. The senators on the Foreign Relations Committee ask the person difficult questions, to find out if he or she is qualified. When Young came before the committee, he gave honest answers. His answers did not always agree with the senators' points of view. Still the Senate committee recommended his appointment, and Young was approved by the full Senate.

On January 31, 1977, Young began his service at the United Nations. To learn more about the world's problems, he took a tour of Africa. While there, he spoke honestly with many African leaders. Some of his views were not popular with the State Department back home, but nobody could doubt his *sincerity*.

Young held his United Nations post for two-and-a-half years. On August 15, 1979, he resigned and looked forward to still another career. Because he is interested in the role of the cities, Young decided to run for mayor of Atlanta. He was elected mayor in 1981. In this post he has continued to display the kind of leadership he was famous for. The post is not an easy one, but he has given it all his energy.

His name still crops up in foreign news. The prime minister of Zimbabwe, Robert Mugabe, visited the United States in September 1983. He made it a point to see an old friend in Atlanta, Andrew Young. They had met in 1977 at the United Nations.

Andrew Young is tall and lean. He looks much younger than he is. He can charm listeners with his smile and manner. He keeps in tiptop physical condition by getting a lot of exercise and watching his diet.

He is a happy family man. On June 7, 1954, he married Jean Childs. She taught at a junior college in Atlanta. They have four children: Andrea, Lisa Dow, Paul Jean, and Andrew Young III.

Who knows what future challenges this man of many roles will accept? No one can deny, at least, that here is a man who has helped to shape the future.

UNDERSTANDING WHAT YOU HAVE READ

Finding Another Title

1. Another good title for this selection might be **(a)** A Leader Known in This Country and Throughout the World **(b)** The Civil-Rights Movement in the United States **(c)** The Importance of the Ambassador to the United Nations **(d)** How Andrew Young Became a Leader in the Civil-Rights Movement.

Getting the Main Idea

2. Andrew Young (a) was an excellent member of Congress (b) knew the great civil-rights leader Dr. Martin Luther King, Jr. (c) has been successful in many different roles (d) has gotten along with people like President Gerald Ford.

Finding Details

3. Andrew Young got his bachelor of science degree in (a) 1932 (b) 1947 (c) 1951 (d) 1955.
4. When Young was hired by the National Council of Churches, he (a) became a minister in Alabama and Georgia (b) worked in a church with a white population (c) ran for Congress (d) moved to New York City.
5. Ralph David Abernathy (a) was a United States senator (b) became leader of Dr. King's civil-rights group (c) ran against Andrew Young in a Georgia election (d) was a dentist in New Orleans.
6. Gerald Ford was chosen to replace (a) Dr. Martin Luther King, Jr. (b) Spiro Agnew (c) Jimmy Carter (d) Andrew Young.
7. The comment that "he believed in a man, not a label" (267) was made about (a) Andrew Young (b) Gerald Ford (c) Dr. Martin Luther King, Jr. (d) Richard Nixon.
8. Young spoke at the Democratic National Convention in (a) 1968 (b) 1970 (c) 1972 (d) 1976.
9. The prime minister of Zimbabwe (a) visited Andrew Young in 1983 (b) opposed Andrew Young's decision to run for mayor (c) was a friend of Gerald Ford (d) helped the election of Jimmy Carter.

10. Young's wife was a former (a) political leader (b) Olympic athlete (c) actress (d) teacher.

Making Inferences

11. Andrew Young worked for a bachelor of science degree because he (a) was an excellent biologist (b) at first wanted to be a dentist (c) especially liked mathematics (d) wanted to become a college teacher.

12. From the mention of Mahatma Gandhi, we may assume that Gandhi (a) was against the civil-rights movement (b) had taught at the Hartford Theological Seminary (c) had used nonviolent protest successfully (d) thought Andrew Young should be mayor of Atlanta.

13. Although Young took a variety of jobs, he was always interested in (a) improving the highways of the United States (b) the civil-rights movement (c) earning a better salary (d) becoming a United States senator.

14. To become a congressman and stay a congressman, Young had to win (a) only one election (b) two elections (c) three elections (d) four elections.

15. When Young supported President Ford's pardon of Richard Nixon, he probably (a) was criticized by many of his friends (b) thought that Ford would appoint him ambassador to the United Nations (c) did it for purely selfish reasons (d) was praised by the black community.

Predicting What Happens Next

16. When he is no longer mayor of Atlanta, Young will probably (a) become a dentist (b) get back his job as ambassador to the United Nations (c) become a minister in a small church (d) seek another job that will challenge him.

Deciding on the Order of Events

17. The following events are scrambled. Arrange them in proper order, as they happened. Use letters only.
    (a) Young gets his bachelor of divinity degree.
    (b) Carter appoints Young to be ambassador to the United Nations.
    (c) Spiro Agnew resigns.
    (d) Young attends Howard University.

Inferring Attitude

18. Andrew Young's attitude (266) toward the black people in poor southern churches is one of (a) annoyance (b) sympathy (c) doubt (d) impatience.

Separating Facts from Opinions

For each of the following, tell whether the statement is a fact (*F*) or an opinion (*O*).
19. When he chose Young for the United Nations post, Carter was showing excellent judgment.
20. Robert Mugabe visited Young in Atlanta.

Understanding Words from Context

21. Many American political leaders are well known in the United States. Far fewer are known *internationally.*
Internationally (265) means **(a)** well **(b)** unfavorably **(c)** at home **(d)** in many countries.

22. He also worked with white leaders to end *segregation,* the forced separation of one race from another.
Segregation (266) means **(a)** keeping groups apart from each other **(b)** finding ways to improve the quality of life **(c)** drawing leaders from different levels of society **(d)** winning friends among the poorer people.

23. The voters approved of his efforts. Two years later he won by a *landslide* victory of 72 percent.
A *landslide* victory (267) is **(a)** unexpected **(b)** disappointing **(c)** impressive **(d)** soon forgotten.

24. He delivered a speech for Carter at the Democratic National Convention in July. He *emphasized* Carter's achievements in civil rights and stressed his concern for blacks.
Emphasized (268) means **(a)** stressed **(b)** overlooked **(c)** disagreed with **(d)** mentioned slightly.

25. While there, he spoke honestly with many African leaders. Some of his views were not popular with the State Department back home, but nobody could doubt his *sincerity.*
Sincerity (269) means **(a)** anger **(b)** irritation **(c)** cleverness **(d)** honesty.

THINKING IT OVER

1. What do you think Andrew Young was seeking when he changed roles so often?
2. How can the government protect the civil rights of all people?
3. Why are some people afraid of other racial groups? How large a part does ignorance play in such fear?
4. Years ago black youths had to go to colleges for blacks. Women, too, were separated. They could not enter colleges like Yale. Now blacks and women can go to schools like Yale. Are these changes for the better? Explain.
5. Peace between nations is sometimes very hard to achieve. How can the United Nations help the cause of world peace?
6. In what areas of the world do you think the United Nations should take a more active role? Explain.
7. What are some of the problems faced by the mayor of a large city like Atlanta?
8. The ambassador to the United Nations represents the president and the United States. Yet the ambassador also has ideas of his or her own to express. How much freedom should an ambassador have in expressing his or her own point of view, if it disagrees with the president's?
9. There are many black governors and other political leaders. In 1984 Jesse Jackson, a black leader, sought the presidential nomination. In that election, a woman, Geraldine Ferraro, actually ran for vice-president. Should our society make it possible for a woman, a black leader, or a member of any minority group to run for president of the United States? Explain.

10. It took courage for Andrew Young to support the nomination of Gerald Ford. Why is it important for senators or members of Congress to think for themselves and not always support their party's line?

ANOTHER LOOK AT THE QUOTATION

> *I have a dream that one day on the red hills of Georgia, the sons of former slaves and the sons of former slave-owners will be able to sit together at the table of brotherhood.*
>
> MARTIN LUTHER KING, JR.

1. Explain the quotation in your own words.
2. How did Martin Luther King, Jr., contribute to world brotherhood?
3. How did Andrew Young try to make King's dream come true?
4. What can individuals and groups do to help make the dream become reality?
5. In light of this quotation, why is it especially fitting that Andrew Young became mayor of Atlanta?

WORDS AT YOUR SERVICE—FUN WITH WORDS

Have you ever played Scrabble? Have you completed a crossword puzzle? Word games like these have always been popular. They have millions of fans. People like to play with words.

One of the most popular of all word games is the anagram. An *anagram* is a word formed from another word or from a bunch of letters chosen at random. If you had the letters *l, v, e,* and *i,* for example, you could make the words *live, evil, vile,* and *veil.*

Sometimes you can rearrange the letters in a word or phrase and come up with an expression that cleverly relates to the original phrase. Here are some famous anagrams:

the eyes	They see.
the countryside	No city dust here.
a decimal point	I'm a dot in place.

A special kind of anagram is the *reversal.* For instance, *ten* spelled backwards is *net. Gnat* spelled backwards is *tang.* Here are some other reversals:

drawer	reward
spots	stops
snap	pans

Another special kind of anagram is the *palindrome.* This is a word or sentence that reads the same backwards and forwards. The name *Anna* is a palindrome. If you turn it around, it still says *Anna.* Here are some other palindromes: *Otto, Hannah, Eve, radar,* and *noon.*

Try your skill at the following:

1. Find the reversal of *remit* and come up with something useful in baking a cake.
2. Exchange just two letters in *united* and come up with a word that means exactly the opposite. (Only two letters have to be changed.)
3. Find the reversal of *stressed* and come up with something that you like at the end of a meal.
4. Make an anagram of *canoe* and come up with a body of water that is much too big for a canoe.
5. Which of the following words are palindromes?
   redder   label   snip   Ava   level

COMPLETING AN OUTLINE

The article on Andrew Young might be outlined in the following way. Five outline items have been omitted. Test your understanding of the structure of the article by following the directions after the outline.

I. Young's early years
   A. Birth in New Orleans
   B. Son of well-to-do family
   C.

II. Schooling
   A. Gilbert Academy
   B. Dillard University
   C.
   D. Hope of becoming a dentist

III. First jobs
   A.
   B. Appointment to churches in white community
   C. His return to the South
   D. Involvement in civil-rights movement

IV. Young's many careers
   A. Work with National Council of Churches
   B. Work with Dr. King and Ralph Abernathy
   C. Election to Congress
   D. Meeting with Carter
   E.
   F. Mayor of Atlanta

V. Andrew Young, the man
   A.
   B. Love of family
   C. The future

Fill in the items omitted from the outline. Correctly match the items in column A with the outline numbers in column B.

A	**B**
1. Appointment as ambassador to United Nations	**a.** I. C.
	b. II. C.
2. Youthful appearance	**c.** III. A.
3. Life in a middle-class neighborhood	**d.** IV. E.
	e. V. A.
4. Ministry	
5. Howard University	

MOTHER TERESA:

Angel of Mercy

*It is better to light one candle than to
curse the darkness.*
    MOTTO OF THE CHRISTOPHER SOCIETY

Calcutta, in India, is a city of wealth and *poverty*, life and death, waste and starvation. There are modern buildings, well-stocked shopping centers, and beautiful houses. There are also terrible slums. Even worse, there are people without even a slum home. In the book *Mother Teresa*, Desmond Doig says, "Nobody really knows, but there are thought to be close to a million pavement dwellers in Calcutta, people who are born on the streets, live on the streets, and die on the streets."

Calcutta is a rich city, filled with beautiful, intelligent people. It is also a poor city, filled with sick and starving people. It was once known as the City of Palaces, but many of the palaces have decayed and become slums. Former Prime Minister Jawaharlal Nehru saw Calcutta as a *"nightmare city."*

Efforts to help Calcutta have not proved enough. The city is hopelessly overcrowded. The overcrowding gets worse every year. In 1947, millions streamed into Calcutta as a result of the division of India. They never left. Every flood or failing harvest in the countryside sends more refugees into the city. Starving farmers leave the land and come to Calcutta. They look for work, but jobs are scarce.

Hopeless people are everywhere, begging for a small sum. Sickness is an everyday matter. Death is a frequent visitor to the streets of Calcutta. The depth of human misery is visible there.

Calcutta's climate adds to the city's difficulties. The heat is always a problem. But the monsoon winds that bring heavy rains between April and October make life especially miserable for street dwellers. Insects and rats prey on the homeless. Malaria, cholera, and other diseases take a deadly toll.

Calcutta has seen many groups of people who tried to help the numerous poor. Government workers have come

and gone. These people have meant well. But most have been forgotten. There is one woman whose name *is* known in Calcutta. Indeed, her name is known around the world. She is Mother Teresa. The story of her life reads like fiction, but all of it is true.

Mother Teresa was born in what is now Yugoslavia on August 27, 1910. Her name was Agnes Gonxha Bojaxhiu. She later took the name *Teresa* after Saint Teresa. She had a sister and a brother. Her father was a grocer.

She attended public school and became interested in religious work in foreign countries. She felt called to help people in need. As she later said, "At the age of 12 I first knew I had a *vocation* to help the poor. I wanted to be a missionary."

Young Agnes had a happy home life. Her dream *conflicted* with her love of home, but the dream won out. At 15 she became interested in working in India. At 18 she joined a community of Irish nuns in Calcutta. This move changed the course of her life.

She taught at St. Mary's High School in Calcutta. She knew very clearly what was happening outside the school walls. She saw the homeless, the sick, and the dying. Her heart went out to these poor forgotten sufferers.

In 1946 Mother Teresa received a "call within a call," as she said later. She felt she had to leave the safety and security of the school. She planned to get some medical training and go into the slums herself. She then went out among the homeless and hopeless, the sick and the dying.

She opened an outdoor school and brought children into it. Volunteers began to help her. Some were her former students. Her group, the Missionaries of Charity, began to grow. All members had to take a vow of poverty. Mother Teresa explained, "To be able to help the poor and know the poor we must be poor ourselves."

She went on, "This vow means that we cannot work for the rich; neither can we accept any money for what we do. Ours is to be a free service and to the poor."

One of the most desperate groups was the lepers. Lepers are seriously diseased people. Since the time of the Bible, lepers have been *outcasts,* avoided by other people. Healthy people have feared catching the disease. Lepers have been treated as already dead and forgotten. Mother Teresa never forgot them, though. She gathered the lepers to her and treated them with medicine and with love.

She has done the same for other seriously ill people. Some of the street people of Calcutta are so ill that they are usually left to die in agony. Mother Teresa gathers these people to her. She has opened a home for the dying poor. Over the years thousands of very sick people who are not welcome anywhere else have come here for treatment and love. Miraculously some have survived. Those who have died have done so surrounded by love.

From her original colony in Calcutta, Mother Teresa's schools, homes, and hospitals have grown. Groups have opened outside Calcutta. In 1959 a home was set up in Drachi. Soon afterward homes were opened in Delhi and then in 22 other cities in India.

Mother Teresa began to spread her message abroad. In the 1960s she left active groups in Sri Lanka, Tanzania, Australia, Venezuela, and Italy. In 1969 Mother Teresa's group was joined with the Missionaries of Charity, a worldwide group. Missionaries of Charity houses opened in Jordan and London, England. Some of her nuns began working in New York City's Harlem. By 1979 there were 158 branches in more than 25 countries.

Wherever there is pain and suffering, Mother Teresa tries to be there. In 1971 she visited Northern Ireland and prayed for peace with Irish women. She met with

Ian Paisley, leader of a warring group. She hoped to heal the wounds.

In 1972 the monsoon winds and rains were particularly bad in Calcutta. Mother Teresa and her helpers waded knee-deep in mud to help rescue slum dwellers from the overflowing sewers. She often risks disease and death in her efforts to aid the poor.

In August 1982 Beirut, the capital of Lebanon, was torn by the worst attacks of the long war there. West Beirut was particularly dangerous. Shells were falling all around. Explosions shattered the air. It was death to move around in that unfortunate area.

Thirty-seven handicapped children lived in that battered section of Beirut. They shivered in terror.

"I am going into West Beirut to rescue those children," Mother Teresa declared.

The authorities told her not to go. "It is too dangerous," they warned her. Mother Teresa disobeyed their orders. She succeeded in finding the children. She said later that she had the permission of the Palestinians—and of the whole world.

In 1984 a deadly gas leak in Bhopal, India, killed thousands. Soon afterward, Mother Teresa was on the scene.

What kind of person is this worker of miracles? She is a small woman, only five feet tall. Her face is wrinkled, but her eyes shine with life. She is sometimes weary with all her efforts, but she always gives the impression of strength. Her smile is warm and friendly.

John E. Frazer, writing for a magazine, said that Mother Teresa has a calm, direct manner. He added that she "can break easily into laughter" but "she can also be *insistent.*" Where the poor are concerned, she will not give up or be controlled by others. She is a well-rounded human being with qualities beyond most people.

Malcolm Muggeridge interviewed Mother Teresa in 1968. During the interview, her face shone with an inner light. He said, "I knew that, even if I were never to see Mother Teresa again, the memory of her would stay with me forever."

The people around her are deeply devoted to her. She has a quality of purity that draws people to her side. She works so hard, but the task is great. As she once said to one of her helpers, "There are so many." She never gives up. Instead, she sighs sadly and then goes on with her work.

Throughout her life Mother Teresa has been given many valuable gifts. She has sold them all and used the money for the poor. When Pope Paul VI visited Mother Teresa in 1964, he gave her his expensive Lincoln Continental car. Mother Teresa had the car auctioned off. With the money she built a colony for lepers in West Bengal.

Many other prizes and awards have come her way. She received the Pope John XXIII Peace Prize in Rome on January 6, 1971. She planned to use the $25,000 cash prize to build a new leper colony.

Later that same year, in October, she was awarded $15,000 by the Joseph Kennedy, Jr., Foundation. She used the money to build a home for the handicapped in Damdam, India. Among her other awards are the Good Samaritan Award, the Jawaharlal Nehru Award, the Templeton Award, and the Presidential Medal of Freedom.

Perhaps the most important award of all is the Nobel Prize for Peace. Ever since it was first given, in 1901, this award has gone to famous political leaders and powerful heads of state. For example, in 1978, Menachem Begin of Israel and Anwar el-Sadat of Egypt shared the award.

In 1979 the award went to Mother Teresa, a person without any political power whatever. In explaining its choice, the Nobel committee spoke of her work among the poor, especially among children and refugees. The announcement also explained that in fighting poverty and distress, Mother Teresa was helping the cause of peace.

A small, modest woman, without armies, can move the world.

UNDERSTANDING WHAT YOU HAVE READ

Finding Another Title

1. Another good title for this selection might be (a) Calcutta: City of Many Moods (b) The Importance of the Nobel Peace Prize (c) A Problem for India (d) Nurse to the Sick and Poor.

Getting the Main Idea

2. To fight the problems of sickness and poverty, one must (a) know the problems firsthand and work unselfishly (b) work closely with governments (c) leave the job to international charities (d) have a lot of political power.

Finding Details

3. India was divided (a) before Mother Teresa was born (b) when Calcutta was 100 years old (c) in 1947 (d) in 1964.

4. Mother Teresa was the daughter of (a) soldier (b) a grocer (c) a religious leader (d) the ruler of Yugoslavia.

5. Mother Teresa first expressed an interest in India when she was (a) 12 (b) 15 (c) 18 (d) 26.

6. Lepers (a) were the only group Mother Teresa would not take in (b) were unknown during biblical times (c) are usually talented (d) have long been avoided by healthy people.

7. The first year mentioned for a home outside Calcutta is (a) 1959 (b) 1964 (c) 1969 (d) 1971.

8. All the following countries have active groups started by Mother Teresa EXCEPT (a) Australia (b) Jordan (c) Greece (d) Italy.

9. Mother Teresa rescued handicapped children in (a) London (b) Ireland (c) Venezuela (d) Lebanon.

10. To build a home for the handicapped in Damdam, India, she used money from (a) the Pope John XXIII Peace Prize (b) the Joseph Kennedy, Jr., Foundation (c) the Templeton Award (d) the Good Samaritan Award.

Making Inferences

11. Pavement dwellers can best be described as people who (a) have stores in the major shopping areas (b) live in houses that are close to the roads (c) have no homes at all (d) beg on the streets by day and stay in small hotels at night.

12. Mother Teresa left home because (a) she felt called to do so (b) of a disagreement with her father (c) she wanted to see the world before she settled down (d) her brother and sister had already left.

13. Mother Teresa left St. Mary's School because she (a) felt she could be more effective outside the walls (b) was offered a better job in New Delhi (c) had disagreements with the other nuns (d) was hired by the Indian government to work among the poor.

14. The influence of Mother Teresa on all her helpers was probably (a) weak (b) strong (c) up and down (d) unimportant.

15. Mother Teresa's action in rescuing the handicapped children can best be described as (a) unimportant (a) selfish (c) courageous (d) ordinary.

Predicting What Happens Next

16. When Mother Teresa visited Bhopal in 1984, she probably (a) blamed everyone in authority for the disaster (b) shook her head sadly and then went home (c) insisted on having her picture taken for the newspapers (d) found ways to help.

Deciding on the Order of Events

17. The following events are scrambled. Arrange them in proper order, as they happened. Use letters only.
    (a) Mother Teresa is awarded the Nobel Peace Prize.
    (b) Mother Teresa comes to India.
    (c) Mother Teresa rescues slum dwellers from the overflowing sewers.
    (d) Mother Teresa goes to Beirut, Lebanon.

Inferring Attitude

18. The attitude of Malcolm Muggeridge (285) toward Mother Teresa is one of (a) love and devotion (b)

surprise and uncertainty (**c**) mild dislike (**d**) fear and worry.

Separating Facts from Opinions

For each of the following, tell whether the statement is a fact *(F)* or an opinion *(O)*.

19. Mother Teresa won the same award that Menachem Begin had previously received.

20. Mother Teresa visited Northern Ireland in the cause of peace.

Understanding Words from Context

21. Calcutta, in India, is a city of wealth and *poverty,* life and death, waste and starvation.
Poverty (281) means the state of being (**a**) careless (**b**) poor (**c**) free (**d**) healthy.

22. She felt called to help people in need. As she later said, "At the age of 12, I first knew I had a *vocation* to help the poor."
Vocation (282) means (**a**) program (**b**) rough idea (**c**) calling (**d**) friend.

23. Her dream *conflicted* with her love of home, but the dream won out.
Conflicted (282) means (**a**) combined (**b**) matched (**c**) met (**d**) clashed.

24. Since the time of the Bible, lepers have been *outcasts,* avoided by other people.
Outcasts (283) are often (**a**) kept apart from society (**b**) leaders of political groups (**c**) kept in special cages (**d**) admitted to churches once a month.

25. He added that she "can break easily into laughter," but "she can also be *insistent.*" Where the poor are concerned, she will not give up or be controlled by others.

    Insistent means **(a)** firm **(b)** easily changed **(c)** cheerful **(d)** quiet.

THINKING IT OVER

1. What special characteristics separate Mother Teresa from most people?
2. Why did she choose to go into the poorest sections of Calcutta to do her work?
3. The government of India does try to help the city of Calcutta. Why is it so hard to make progress?
4. It is easy to love good, healthy, sweet people. Should we also love those who do not have wonderful characteristics? Explain.
5. What does Mother Teresa get from all the difficulties she has to go through?
6. Have you ever done an unselfish thing that no one else knew about? How did you feel?
7. Why did the Nobel committee award a *peace* prize to Mother Teresa? Do you agree with the committee's choice? Why or why not?

ANOTHER LOOK AT THE QUOTATION

> *It is better to light one candle than curse the darkness.*
> MOTTO OF THE CHRISTOPHER SOCIETY

1. Explain the quotation in your own words.
2. Do you believe that the idea of the quotation is a good one? Why or why not?
3. Did Mother Teresa light some candles? Explain.

WORDS AT YOUR SERVICE—VIVID, SPECIFIC WORDS

> *Former Prime Minister Jawaharlal Nehru saw Calcutta as a "nightmare city." (281)*

Notice how vivid, or strong, the expression *nightmare city* is. We have all experienced frightening dreams. Therefore the word *nightmare* brings to mind strong feelings. If Nehru had said *unhappy city* or *sad city,* the description would not be so powerful.

In your own writing, try to use words that make pictures. For instance, if you write the sentence "The proud old man *walked* along," you send a message. But you could make your message much more vivid by substituting one of these words for *walked: hobbled, marched, stumbled, strolled, shuffled,* or *limped.*

In each of the following sentences, choose the word that you think makes the best picture. Tell why.
1. Our homesick new puppy (cried, whimpered) all night.
2. "Why don't you watch out where you're going!" the angry motorist (said, snarled).
3. I enjoy playing (basketball, sports).

4. On top of the mountain there was a beautiful old (oak tree, tree).

5. When I arrived at the front door, two (dogs, poodles) came bouncing up to me.

Point out which sentence in each of the following pairs is more effective. Tell why.

6. a. Tonight we're having my favorite dessert.
   b. Tonight we're having chocolate pudding with whipped cream.

7. a. Dad planted some vegetables and fruits.
   b. Dad planted tomatoes, green beans, lettuce, and strawberries.

8. a. The first three hikers scrambled upward to reach the summit first.
   b. The first three hikers walked ahead of us.

9. a. Three cats won ribbons at the cat show.
   b. A Persian, a Siamese, and a calico cat all won ribbons at the show.

10. a. My brother collects tickets to plays, movies, circuses, and sports events.
    b. My brother has an unusual collecting hobby.

COMPLETING AN OUTLINE

The article on Mother Teresa might be outlined in the following way. Five outline items have been omitted. Test your understanding of the structure of the article by following the directions after the outline.

I. Calcutta
   A. Wealth and poverty
   B.
   C. Need for help
   D. Work of Mother Teresa

II. Mother Teresa's early years
   A. Birth and family
   B.
   C. Teaching in Calcutta
   D. Work with the poor and the sick
   E. Vows of poverty

III. Travels and accomplishments
   A. Growth of influence beyond Calcutta
   B. Travels to many countries
   C. Attempt to bring peace to Northern Ireland
   D. Help with the flooding in Calcutta
   E.

IV. Mother Teresa herself
   A. Appearance
   B.
   C. Devotion of her helpers
   D. Sadness and determination

V. Prizes and awards
   A. Gift of Pope Paul VI
   B. Awards by many countries
   C.

Fill in the items omitted from the outline. Correctly match the items in column A with the outline numbers in column B.

A	**B**
1. Interest in missionary work	a. I. B.
2. Crowded conditions	b. II. B.
3. The Nobel Peace Prize	c. III. E.
4. Personal qualities	d. IV. B.
5. Rescue of children in West Beirut	e. V. C.

UNIT 5

ANOTHER LOOK

HOW MUCH DO YOU REMEMBER?

1. The person who received the Nobel Peace Prize is (a) Margaret Thatcher (b) Andrew Young (c) Mother Teresa (d) Joseph Kennedy, Jr.
2. All the following are correctly matched EXCEPT (a) Andrew Young—Atlanta (b) Mahatma Gandhi—India (c) Mother Teresa—Calcutta (d) Margaret Thatcher—Lebanon.
3. The person who was born in what is now Yugoslavia is (a) Jawharlal Nehru (b) Pope Paul VI (c) Mother Teresa (d) Spiro Agnew.
4. The person most closely associated with civil rights is (a) Edward Heath (b) Andrew Young (c) Henry Ford (d) Mother Teresa.
5. The two countries that fought over the Falkland Islands are (a) Great Britain and India (b) Argentina and India (c) Great Britain and Argentina (d) none of these.
6. Margaret Thatcher belongs to the (a) Liberal party (b) Labour party (c) Conservative party (d) Republican party.
7. The word that best describes the city of Calcutta is (a) overcrowded (b) cold (c) modern (d) rural.
8. The person who never got involved in politics is (a) Luis Muñoz Marín (b) Andrew Young (c) Margaret Thatcher (d) Mother Teresa.

9. The person who worked with Dr. King's civil-rights group is **(a)** Margaret Thatcher **(b)** Andrew Young **(c)** Spiro Agnew **(d)** Mother Teresa.
10. The person who worked closely with Martin Luther King, Jr., is **(a)** Mother Teresa **(b)** Gerald Ford **(c)** Andrew Young **(d)** Richard Nixon.

WHAT IS YOUR OPINION?

1. Which of the two leaders in this unit worked most closely and personally with poor people? What help did they provide?
2. If you had the chance to meet one leader in this unit, which one would you choose? Explain.
3. Which person in this unit made the most permanent contribution to humanity? Defend your choice.
4. Choose one person in the unit. Show how he or she was true to himself or herself.
5. Would you like to be a leader like one of the people in this unit? Explain your attitude.

THE QUOTATION AND THE UNIT

Steady nerves and a quiet mind are not things we go out and find; they are things we create.
JOHN R. MILLER

1. Explain the quotation in your own words.
2. Do you agree with the point of the passage? Explain.
3. Do you think the subjects in this unit had to develop steady nerves?
4. Sometimes the greatest satisfaction in life comes from helping others. Which subject in the unit might get the greatest satisfaction from his or her work? Defend your choice.